Breakthrough

Living a Life That

OVERFLOWS

Breakthrough

Living a Life That
OVERFLOWS

RABBI JASON SOBEL

RJS Publishing

Breakthrough: Living a Life That Overflows

Copyright © 2020 by Rabbi Jason Sobel

ISBN: 978-1-7348071-0-3

Front cover image by KevinCarden/Lightstock.

Printed by Sheridan.

First printing edition 2020.

RJS Publishing
5062 Lankershim Blvd., Suite 3017
North Hollywood, CA 91601

www.fusionglobal.org
For information about purchasing this title in bulk please email info@fusionglobal.org.

Table of Contents

Jason's Journey

I GREW UP A nice Jewish boy from a good, conservative family in Springfield, New Jersey. I was raised going to Hebrew school but did not want to follow the religious rhetoric of my traditional upbringing. I wanted to know this God who the Bible describes as a "consuming fire" (Hebrews 12:29). I had to go on my quest to discover if God was real. I wanted a living, breathing encounter with the God of creation.

Being Jewish was extremely important to the Sobel household. After all, our family was a living legacy of Holocaust survivors. Most of my mom's relatives died during the Holocaust, so being Jewish was always something deeply ingrained in the very fibers of my being. I grew up with this rich understanding of my identity as a Jew. I had a keen awareness of the need to support the state of Israel, and a love for my Jewish traditions permeated my core identity.

I am not sure if it is humanly possible for a child to enjoy the rigors and religious rituals of Hebrew school. However, I regularly attended Hebrew school as a child. I prepared for my bar mitzvah at the age of thirteen, attending synagogue every Saturday morning and reading Hebrew scrolls. My family wasn't quite *Fiddler on the Roof*, but we were a family of strong faith and traditions. Of course, all this was still secondary to basketball and the number one priority of hanging out with my friends.

After being unfairly kicked off the school basketball team, I went looking for new friends in all the wrong places. I became close friends with a hip-hop DJ. At seventeen years of age, I wound up dropping out of high school, partying with a rough crowd in New York City, and getting in trouble with my wanna-be gang friends. After staring danger in the face one too many times, I left that life. I earned an engineering internship at a large recording studio in New York City, where many rock and rap stars recorded. Looking at their lives full of fame and fortune, I saw how unhappy and dysfunctional they and their families were.

I realized I needed something different and something more, and that's when I began my spiritual quest. My best friend, John, introduced me to the martial arts and Eastern philosophy. I began studying and reading Eastern philosophy and religion. Through the process of unanswered questions leading to more questions, I became a "Jew-Bu," a Jewish Buddhist. I was looking for meaning and purpose, and had a hunger and a thirst for the divine and spiritual power in my life. I was willing to travel to the ends of the earth to discover this: *Is there a God? For what purpose am I created? Is there more in life than fame and fortune?*

Like a man on a mission, I set my heart on a pilgrimage journey through the unending maze of unanswered questions, which seemed to fill every waking moment. I became very involved with a Jewish New Age teacher who introduced me to the spiritual practices of Eastern Mysticism.

I gave myself wholeheartedly to pursuing an encounter with God through the study of both Judaism and New Age practices. I began sleeping on the floor of my house, became a strict vegetarian, and dreamed of my epic pilgrimage to India.

One day while meditating for hours a day and spending large amounts of time studying the teachings of great spiritual masters from India and the East, I had the spiritual encounter I was seeking. Suddenly, my body began to shake and vibrate violently. I felt a new energy and raw power course through my veins. Perhaps this sounds dramatic to you, but I promise that this experience was authentic. My spirit began to lift out of my body. In this transcendental state, I remember looking down, and I could see my physical body sitting there on the floor. At the same time, I felt my spirit floating up and rising higher and higher.

I went through the roof of my house. I began to fly into the clouds and continued to go up. The next thing I knew, I was in heaven standing before a glorious throne. Seated on this stunning throne unlike anything I had ever seen, read about, or could scarcely imagine, was Yeshua-Jesus. You may be asking yourself, *How could a nice Jewish boy from Jersey know who Jesus was?* Honestly, there was something deep inside me that just knew. To this date, it was the best experience of my life. The encounter was unmatchable in every way and the experience of a lifetime.

My body was vibrating and radiating with energy, power, and a deep, abiding undercurrent of complete peace. I was in a state of bliss and euphoria. As I stood before my Maker, moments somehow seemed to slow into eternity. A day can indeed be like one thousand years, and a moment can feel like a lifetime.

Finally, the Lord spoke to me, and I will never forget His words. He said, "Many are called, but few are chosen."

I said, "Lord, am I chosen?"

He sweetly smiled and replied, "Yes."

The next thing I knew, I was no longer in heaven. That euphoric bliss still covered me almost like a light down blanket, but I was instantly back in my body in my bedroom. I sat in my room again, shrouded with a complete sense of *shalom* (peace) and joy. A peace that surpasses all understanding filled the marrow of my bones, the cells of my being, and the cavities of my soul. This filling kept me in this state of blissful, perfect peace and deep contentment. So energized, I ran down the steps and outside into my front yard. I ran around in circles, jumping up and down, screaming at the top of my lungs, "I am called to serve Him, I am called to serve Him!"

Just at this moment, my mom pulled up into the driveway and saw her good little Jewish son running around in circles like a crazy man for all the neighbors to gawk at. Surely, she thought I was *mashugana* (a Yiddish term describing a person who is nonsensical, silly, or crazy). I didn't care, as I was so elated, ecstatic, excited, and enamored by the fact that God wanted to use me. Finite words pale in comparison to the reality of the emotions pulsating behind that experience.

> A peace that surpasses all understanding filled the marrow of my bones, the cells of my being, and the cavities of my soul. This filling kept me in this state of blissful, perfect peace and deep contentment.

Although she did not understand what was happening to me, my mother did not want to rain on my parade. There was only one problem. I wondered, *What does it look like for a nice Jewish boy to begin serving Yeshua?* I had no clue.

Shortly after my unearthly experience, I was walking down the street for several hours after practicing yoga in a Soho, New York, ashram. The shirt I had on said TRUTH on the front. A woman coming from the opposite direction approached me. She said, "Can I ask you a question?"

I said, "Sure."

She asked me, "What is the truth? Do you think the truth is clear and absolute and that easy to understand in the world in which we are living?"

Her questions blew me away because they were more or less what my shirt said *on the back*. There was no way she could read what was on the back of my shirt. All of a sudden, she began to gaze *through* me. I became mesmerized and fixated upon her. It was like time began to freeze slowly and I really couldn't say anything. It was as if we were in a bubble, and all that existed was the two of us. Everything around us began to fade away.

She proceeded to tell me about the truth, about how Yeshua-Jesus was the truth, the way, and the life. Energy and power radiated from her that kept me fixed in that spot. I could not move or speak. All I could do was listen to every word she was saying.

The next thing I knew, no one was standing in front of me. It was a crazy spiritual experience. I don't know if she was an angel or what she was, but I remember thinking to myself, *There's something about this Yeshua, this Jesus. I've encountered Him meditating. Now I've encountered Him through this person on the street.* Something again went off in my mind: I needed to find out who He was, not what New Age teachers or secondary writings in books said about Him. Who did He say He was? Who was this Yeshua whom I encountered face-to-face, and what did He teach? What did He want from my life?

By this time, my friend John had become a believer in Yeshua, and he would try to share about it with me as often as possible. One day, he called me on the telephone and asked, "You went to Hebrew school as a child, right? Do you think you could tell the difference between the Old and New Testament if I read you some passages?"

I said, "Sure."

He read me the passage of this guy dying on the cross and asked if it was Old or New Testament.

I said, "Obviously, it's the New Testament, because it's talking about Jesus."

He read another passage: "He was pierced for our transgressions; He was crushed for our iniquities . . . He was led like a lamb to the slaughter." Then he asked, "Is this the Old or New Testament?"

I said, "It must be the New Testament, because it sounds like it's talking about Jesus."

John paused, then said, "It's from the Old Testament, from Isaiah 53. Isaiah was a Jewish prophet who lived seven hundred years before Messiah was born."

This fact got my attention and began to provoke me to envy. Later I would learn that the Apostle Paul used the word *envy* to describe how I was feeling. He wrote in Romans 11:14, "In the hope that I may somehow arouse my own people to envy and save some of them" (NIV).

After our conversation, I agreed to go with John to the messianic synagogue led by Rabbi Jonathan Cahn, who would later write the highly acclaimed and best-selling book *The Harbinger*. My friend prayed to lead one Jewish person to faith, but he never thought it would be me. He didn't know it would be possible.

The music and message at the synagogue were excellent, and I enjoyed the evening. Then the room lights dimmed and they began to pray. I figured I needed all the help I could get. I was looking for spiritual enlightenment, so I was more than happy to pray.

It was the first time I had ever prayed to Yeshua-Jesus, and the people asked, "Those whose first time it was to pray to Jesus, please raise your hands."

I raised my hand.

> I had read the New Testament and believed that Jesus was the one that Moses and the prophets had foretold. He was the one who spoke the words of eternal life.

They continued, "If you have raised your hand, please stand up. You've just been born anew."

I had no idea what it meant to be born anew, but I knew it was something a nice Jewish boy should never do. God knows what would happen if I were born again. I gave my mother enough trouble when I was born once. So I decided not to stand.

Suddenly, a man from Brooklyn said to me, "I saw you raise your hand. If you can't stand here for the Messiah, you won't be able to stand for Him in the world."

I didn't want to make a scene, so I stood up. They brought me to meet with one of the leaders, who began to tell me about the decision I had made. Rabbi Jonathan Cahn led me in a prayer to receive Yeshua. Then they gave me the first New Testament that I had ever seen.

I took it home, not quite sure about what had just happened. I hid it in my room, and God forbid that my parents should find it. Of course, Mom found it and confronted me, "What is this? Don't tell me you're a Jew who believes in Jesus?"

However, I had read the New Testament and believed that Jesus was the one that Moses and the prophets had foretold. He was the one who spoke the words of eternal life. My mom was concerned for me and called our rabbi to meet with me. Knowing I was going to face the rabbi, I knew I had to do further study to verify for myself that Yeshua was the Messiah of the Hebrew Bible. I listed all the messianic promises and prophecies in the Hebrew Scriptures, and I studied in preparation to meet with the rabbi.

The rabbi asked me how I came to believe in Yeshua as Messiah, and I read through all the passages that impacted me. For instance, Daniel 9 talks about when the Messiah was going to come. I pointed out that all the calculations in this chapter point to the time when Yeshua walked the earth. The rabbi researched Daniel and got back to me. He refuted my arguments and said that Daniel was full of metaphors and was an apocalyptic book. He said not to calculate from this book, and he who does brings a curse upon himself. The only bearing the meeting with the rabbi had on me was it gave me a greater hunger and desire to study Messianic Judaism.

I found a school that had a messianic Jewish program. There, I attended summer school after being a follower of

Yeshua for only four months and decided to stay for further studies. During my time there, I realized that Yeshua-Jesus came to make *better* Jews. All of the prophets foretold that the Messiah would bring the Jewish people back to covenantal faithfulness, and strengthen their commitment to Jewish life and their calling to the people of Israel. As a result of my newfound faith, my Jewish identity increased tremendously. Suddenly, everything I had done as a child growing up had profound spiritual significance. I found I had a deeper connection with and understanding of who the Messiah was and what He came to do.

God began to work in new and powerful ways in my life. He said to me, "It's not enough to tell people that God loves them. You need to tangibly show the love, presence, and power of God by praying for people, and watch the Kingdom of God break into this age by bringing healing and wholeness into lives." I felt God bringing me back to the power I had experienced initially when I first came to know Him.

One week after coming to faith, I received a phone call from Jeff, a homeless friend in New York City. He had been sleeping on the streets on a cold winter night in Chinatown, and his legs had become frostbitten overnight. He was hospitalized in NYU Medical Center, scared to death that he would not walk again. What did I know? I had read the Gospels and the book of Acts. I thought, *We can do what they did.*

John and I went to the hospital to visit him. I had the faith to pray for people and believed that God would make them whole. Jeff was downcast and distraught. His legs were blackish and green. I said, "Jeff, I'm going to pray for you, and I believe that God can heal you." I laid my hands on him and echoed the words of Peter (Acts 3:6), who said, "Silver and gold have I none, but what I have, in the name of Yeshua I say rise, take up your bed and walk." A couple of days later, Jeff walked out of the hospital on perfect legs.

I knew that this shouldn't be a one-time experience but a normal way of life for followers of Yeshua. I began to step out in faith and pray for healing for people to show the love of God for them. I've seen supernatural manifestations of God's presence and power since that day with Jeff. The Apostle Paul says clearly that his teaching didn't come by wise and persuasive words (1 Corinthians 2:4). It comes with the convincing proof of the Spirit's power so that faith doesn't rest upon the wisdom of men but on the power of God.

Close to fifteen years after coming to know the Lord, I felt God calling me to California. Nine months after moving to Los Angeles, I was invited to a conference on healing. While at the conference, God spoke to me and told me that I was going to go through a season of Joseph. I felt the still voice of God saying to me that I would go through pits and prisons that would be used to purify and humble me for the more significant promise of breakthrough that the Lord had for me. I had no idea at the time what that would mean.

Less than a year later, I was fired from what I thought was my dream ministry job, which had caused my move to Los Angeles. I had no job and struggled to pay the bills. Things were tough on a financial level, but spiritually I was developing a deeper intimacy with the Lord. I spent a year praying and pursuing the Lord. God miraculously provided during this season. He began to open incredible new doors for me. But I also experienced a lot of loss and challenges. I saw glimpses of breakthrough and saw some of the promises come to pass, but they were only partial.

Three years ago, Kathie Lee Gifford called me on the phone and told me she was working on a new book and wanted to meet and talk about my involvement with the project. I flew to NYC, and after we had lunch, she asked me to help her write the book *The Rock, the Road, and the Rabbi*, which went on to become a *New York Times* best seller. I thought this was the start of the significant breakthrough God had promised. In truth, it was the start—it laid the foundation—but it was not yet the time to see the fuller fruition. There were still some problems and pains that I needed to experience in preparation for what the Lord wanted to do.

A major turning point occurred in the fall of 2019. Heading into the new Hebrew year of 5780, the Lord began to speak to me about this decade being the decade of breakthrough. The number eighty is connected with breakthrough, as we will explore further in the pages ahead. September 29, 2019 was Rosh Hashanah, the Jewish New Year, which began the new year of 5780, the decade of divine strength and breakthrough. Starting on the Jewish New Year, I not only spoke about breakthrough, but so many of the things God spoke to me about throughout the years began coming to pass in an accelerated way.

Our Rosh Hashanah service had close to one thousand people in attendance. It was our biggest ever. Shawn Bolz, a good friend of mine, also shared, and the message the Lord gave him for the season focused on breakthrough as well. The Lord had given him the same word *breakthrough* before he ever knew about the significance of the Hebrew year.

That evening God put in people's hearts to partner with us and support us in ways that had been needed for years to grow Fusion as a ministry and to increase our impact. Several months earlier, God had spoken to me about building our team. For years there had just been a few of us, but the Lord allowed us to do a lot with a little. A few months after the decade of breakthrough began, we had breakthrough in building the team. We now have several new team members, and our impact and reach are greater than ever.

I had also dreamed about creating more resources to help people with their hunger to delve deeper into the Scriptures and the Jewish roots of their faith. But I didn't have the bandwidth, or the various pieces needed to produce them, with excellence. All that changed as we moved in this decade. This book, along with two others, are in the works. One of them will be published with a major publisher who is very excited to work with us. On our website, we also launched a weekly

"Guide to the Torah" reading and are planning on filming several more online classes.

God is also bringing breakthroughs in the area of media. Daystar TV invited me to appear on several shows. One show is a special on Israel and the end times with a panel of other spiritual leaders that included Rabbi Jonathan Cahn, Pastor Jimmy Evan of Gateway Church Dallas, Pastor Troy Brewer, and Shawn Bolz. In January of 2020, I filmed a show with Matt and Lori Crouch for *Praise* on TBN. All of this is leading to even more media opportunities. Our media breakthroughs also include the launch of two apps and some potential new projects with Kathie Lee Gifford that will be completed this year.

There is so much more to tell on a personal and ministry level. God is opening amazing doors and bringing breakthrough in incredible ways. It's taken much more than a decade for me to see the promise of breakthrough that the Lord promised, but I am experiencing it now. And what the Lord did is doing for me, He wants to do for you. It's time for breakthrough.

Introduction

WE ARE STARTING a new decade and a new year on the biblical Hebrew calendar. According to the Hebrew calendar, this is the year 5780, and this year comes with life-changing significance that I will cover in this book.

The Hebrew civil New Year is a significant time for Jews. But it is interesting for us to know that Jewish tradition tells us that the birth of creation, Sarah's conception of Isaac, and Joseph's release from the palace all occurred at this time of the year.

Before we take a look at this upcoming year, let me explain a bit about the establishment of the Hebrew calendar. In traditional Judaism there are several New Years, four to be exact. The most well-known is *Tishrei*, which is the start of the civil new year or "the year for the season" and is also the anniversary (or birthday) of creation (Rosh Hashanah). It's also the New Year for the counting of Sabbatical years and the Jubilee.

Hillel the Elder ratified the modern Jewish calendar in the third century AD. The sages determined four separate New Year dates. Tishrei (Rosh Hashanah) is the first. The second new year is *Shevat*, the New Year for trees. "Most Jewish sources consider 15 Shevat as the New Year both for designating fruits as *orlah* (that is, forbidden to eat, because they have grown during the first three years after a tree's planting) and for separating fruits for tithing."[1] The third Jewish New Year is 1 *Nisan*. It corresponds to the season of redemption from Egypt and the birth of the nation Israel. The fourth and last new year is 1 *Elul*. It is the new year for tithing cattle.

The civil calendar begins in the September–October period. New Year's Day in the civil year is called Rosh Hashanah, or the beginning of the year, and it falls on the seventh month of the religious calendar. Passover (March–April) marks the beginning of the religious calendar for counting the Jewish festivals and also the New Year for the rule of Jewish kings (Exodus 12:1–2). The cycles of the moon, not the sun, is the basis of the Hebrew calendar, as the Egyptian calendar focused on their god of Ra (the sun god). God wanted the Israelites to not only escape from the bondage and slavery of Egypt but to also move away from any form of idol or false god worship, so He told them to create something new to track the months and years.

From my understanding, Tishrei was historically considered to be the first month of the Hebrew calendar, but the Exodus was such a defining spiritual and national event that

---

1 Michelle Alperin, "How Many Jewish New Years?" *My Jewish Learning*, https://www.myjewishlearning.com/article/how-many-jewish-new-years/.

was so foundational in shaping the identity and destiny of Israel that Nisan was named the beginning of the religious calendar. It is very similar to how Christians reset the calendar and dating of time in relation to the death of Yeshua—who died on Passover. Like the Exodus, this event was such a world-changing and history-defining spiritual event that a revised calendar needed to be created for Christians.

Rosh Hashanah ("the head of the year") is associated with the Feast of Ingathering (Exodus 23:16). It is a designated time of repentance. Rosh Hashanah begins the ten days that climax in Yom Kippur, or Day of Atonement.

According to Dr. Faydra Shapiro in her book *Romance Behind Judaica:*

> *[Rosh Hashanah] offers a chance for healthy personal introspection and spiritual recommitment. Second, as the official beginning of the Jewish New Year, it signals the opportunity to wipe the slate clean and make a fresh start. Third, according to one Jewish tradition, God created humans on this day. This makes Rosh Hashanah a birthday celebration for humanity.*[2]

This past Rosh Hashanah ushered in the year 5780 as well as a new decade for us. Why 5780? The Jewish calendar

---

2   Faydra L. Shapiro, Ph.D., with Len Woods, *Romance Behind Judaica: Celebrating the Richness of the Jewish Calendar* (New York: Worthy/Hachette Book Group, 2019), 113.

counts the years from the creation of the world (according to Jewish biblical tradition); therefore, the year, according to Jewish tradition, is 5780.

The year of 5780 is important for us, and we'll explore the significance of the upcoming decade. The new decade brings the opportunity for a new season for us. In the following pages, we will learn that this decade is a time for us to "see and say." We'll also discover this decade is a time of breakthrough for us—a season for us to break through any barriers that hold us back from being all that God has called us to be and living in the overflow.

I'm excited to share with you how God is leading us to a new season. Are you ready?

BREAKING THROUGH TO A LIFE THAT OVERFLOWS

I wrote this book so all of us could understand how we can break through the barriers that keep us from experiencing God's best in our lives. We will dive deeply into what breakthrough means and how we can join God in His plans for us to break free and do what He's called us to do.

The second part of this book will help you go beyond breakthrough to living a life of overflow. Yeshua-Jesus came to give us a full, abundant life (John 10:10). To help you see how you can achieve this full life, we will take a deep dive into Yeshua's first miracle, the miracle at Cana in John 2. From understanding this miracle, you will learn how you can not only break through but also clearly live the John 10:10 promised life.

We are excited to have you with us on this adventure into new and exciting ways to live our lives as believers in the Messiah. We are grateful for the opportunity to minister, teach, and learn with you.

Shalom,
Rabbi Jason

PART 1: BREAKTHROUGH

BEFORE WE BEGIN

THIS FIRST SECTION will introduce two concepts that will give a better understanding as you move forward to your breakthrough and life in the overflow. We begin by looking at the importance of times and seasons in our lives. Judaism is embedded in time and seasons. Jews celebrated on specific days in a yearly cycle of feast, fast, and celebration. This cycle gave them a clear understanding of history as well as the present and future.

Before we begin, we also need to understand some aspects of the Hebrew language. One facet of the Hebrew alphabet is that each letter also has a numerical value. You'll need to understand this as we venture into the importance of this decade and the idea of a breakthrough.

ALIGNING THE TIMES AND THE SEASONS

We meet some intriguing people in 1 Chronicles 12:33: "From the sons of Issachar—men who know how to interpret the signs of the times to determine what Israel should do—200 chiefs with all their kinsmen under their command." The sons of Issachar understood the times, and they knew what to do. It's interesting that with understanding came the knowledge of what to do.

I believe understanding the times is essential. We need to be aware of what is happening around us. We need understanding so we know what to do. These men understood the affairs of the day. They knew their culture, and they had the wisdom to know what was going to happen in the future. Their allegiance was with King Saul, while he was alive, and yet they fully understood that David's time was coming. When the conditions changed (Saul died, and so did his commander, Abner), they changed their allegiance to David, their new king. Times are crucial, and understanding the times and the seasons is critical for us. The times and the seasons are woven into the fabric of creation; from the very beginning, God ordained the times and seasons for us. It's our responsibility, like the sons of Issachar, to understand the times and know what to do. Bible scholar Alan Redpath, commenting on the sons of Issachar, wrote:

> *Bless your heart, this is God's time! What is He teaching you now? Mother, father, brokenhearted friend, even if you are living in the midst of frustration, it is God's time. May He give you an understanding of it!*[3]

---

3   Alan Redpath, *The Making of a Man of God: Lessons from the Life of David* (Grand Rapids, MI: Revell, 2004).

This year, 5780, gives us a fresh way to align to a new decade. With God's help we can understand the time and know what to do with His leading and guiding into fresh areas of our life we call breakthroughs.

UNDERSTANDING NUMBERS AND LETTERS

As we dive deeper into understanding the times, seasons, and breakthroughs, we need to discover some things about Hebrew letters and numbers. For example, Rosh Hashanah is a time of creation. Jewish sages teach that the first Rosh Hashanah was the sixth day of creation. The sixth day is the day of creation, as this was the day God created man and woman (Genesis 1:24–31). The sixth day is a day of remembrance of when God created us. So we confess to God on the day we were created—the day God spoke us into existence, the sixth day.

> Times are crucial, and understanding the times and the seasons is critical for us. The times and the seasons are woven into the fabric of creation; from the very beginning, God ordained the times and seasons for us.

The Hebrew language is alphanumeric, as numbers are written by letters. Letters and numbers are interchangeable in Hebrew. When God spoke the world into existence, He created the heavens and the earth. When He created the spiritual aspects of creation, He used words. All things are held together by His word. Hebrews 1:3 tells us, "This Son is the radiance of His glory and the imprint of His being, upholding all things by His powerful word."

Likewise, the psalmist tells us, "By ADONAI's word were the heavens made, and all their host by the breath of His mouth" (Psalm 33:6). His word undergirds the spiritual reality, and that same word in Hebrew has a numerical value attached to it. Therefore, underlying the physical reality of creation is the number behind God's Word and the very mathematical structure of creation. God is the original programmer. He spoke the world into existence, and each spoken word represented a number. In doing that, He created the "code of creation." God created the Matrix, not Neo.

There's a code behind creation (spiritual and physical) that involves letters and numbers. Therefore, words and numbers are both significant. Here's an example:

The first word of Genesis 1 is the word *Bereshit*, "in the beginning." The first letter of *Bereshit* is *bet*. When you look at the letter, it appears to be a house. The *be* of *bet* has a numerical value of two. So the first letter in the Bible has a numerical value of two. Why? Because God created the world in twos. He created heaven and earth. He created light and dark. He created day and night. He created the sun and the moon. He created the sea and the dry ground. He created man and woman. What's interesting is only when the two (man and women, day and night, and the rest) work in alignment can another *bet* or blessing (*Bracha* in Hebrew) be released. God created the world, and you in particular, for blessing. However, for this blessing there needs to be alignment. God created the world to bless it because both words (*beginning* and *blessing*) start with the same *bet*.

Bereshit can also be read "in the firstborn (or through the firstborn), God created world." *Bet* is a picture of the world and the world existing in the firstborn Son, Yeshua-Jesus. In Him we live and move and have our being (Acts 17:28). It is interesting that the first letter of Genesis is the Hebrew letter *bet*, and the last word of the book of Revelation is the Hebrew word *amen*, which ends in the letter *nun*. The first and last letters of the Bible spell the Hebrew word *Ben*, which means "son." Here's the significance: From the very first letter to the very last letter, everything in the Bible points to the Son, Yeshua.

Our God is a wonderful, awe-inspiring God. From a scientific perspective, how can we say that God spoke the world into existence? When we read the Bible and understand the Hebrew language of words, letters, and numbers, we find quantum physics and a mathematical structure to the universe. The biblical narrative is a beautiful story because the ancients could not comprehend the science behind how the world began, but God inspired them to create a language that thoroughly explained it.

1

A Decade of Supernatural Strength and Breakthrough

THE YEAR **5780** begins the decade of supernatural strength and breakthrough. Consonants represent dates in Hebrew. The consonant for *eighty* is the seventeenth letter of the twenty-two-letter Hebrew alphabet: *Peh* is both a word and letter. It means "mouth." If you examine the letter *peh*, you will see that it looks like the profile of a face, with a nose and a mouth and

Peh

a *dagesh* (a "dot" for an eye). If you look at the white space within the letter, there's a *bet* inside the letter *peh* (we'll talk more about this later). What this all tells us is 5780 is the decade of the mouth.

Psalm 81:10 says, "I am the LORD your God, who brought you up out of Egypt. Open wide your mouth and I will fill it" (NIV). The first part reminds us of Exodus 19 and the "elevating" of Israel out of the bondage in Egypt. The conclusion of the verse tells us of the wide-open mouths of baby birds as they eagerly await food from their mother. Their mouths (peh) are wide open to receive nourishment as well as to speak of what they need. During the decade of the mouth, we need to be ready for God's nourishment, and also be prepared to declare the breakthroughs He is doing for us.

> According to the Psalms and Jewish tradition, eighty is associated with strength. God will give us the strength to overcome the inner as well as the outer obstacles and oppositions that we are going to face during these times.

Nehemiah 8:10 reminds us that the joy of the Lord is our strength. There's an understanding in Jewish thought that says, "Joy breaks through every yoke." The Hebrew expression is *simcha poretz geder*. The expression *breaks through* begins with the letter *peh* and is the same word for *breakthrough*. If, as Nehemiah tells us, the Lord's joy is my strength, then He's waiting for me to ask Him for it so I can break through anything that is holding me back from living the life He wants for me (see also Psalm 27:1; 2 Samuel 22:33; and 2 Corinthians 12:9–10).

The word for *breakthrough* in Hebrew is *peres*. "It refers to a rupture, a breaking up or shattering of something; a breach created in a wall of an enemy (2 Samuel 5:20); the breaking or rupture occurring in the process of childbirth (Genesis 38:29)."[4] The word *peres* begins with the letter *peh*. This decade is the decade of the mouth as well as a decade of strength (*gevurah*) and breakthrough (peres). In the next section, we will explain how these terms are connected in letters and numbers. What is most critical for us to remember is God wants to strengthen us for our breakthrough.

EIGHTY AND STRENGTH: TWO EXAMPLES

Psalm 90:10 tells us, "The span of our years is seventy—or with strength, eighty—yet at best they are trouble and sorrow. For they are soon gone, and we fly away." According to the psalmist, an average lifespan is seventy, but we can go beyond seventy to eighty. Gevurah is the strength necessary to overcome the inner and outer obstacles and opposition we face. According to the Psalms and Jewish tradition, eighty is associated with strength. God will give us the strength to overcome the inner as well as the outer obstacles and oppositions that we are going to face during these times. Remember the children of Issachar? They had godly strength to discern the times and wisdom to understand the seasons of life. A key to understanding these times is knowing the strength we have available to us to overcome.

---

4   Barry Jenkins Sr., "Getting Your Breakthrough," *A Daily Word*, February 21, 2001, https://pastorblj.blogspot.com/2011/02 /getting-your-breakthrough.html.

Moses

Moses was eighty years old when God strengthened him to lead the children of Israel out of Egypt. God gave Moses a new strength to perform a divine mission and calling at eighty years old. He was the peh (eighty). Moses' new strength included not merely physical strength and stamina, but also the strength to overcome his fears. Moses expressed his anxieties in Exodus 4:10, saying, "ADONAI, I am not a man of words—not yesterday, nor the day before, nor since You have spoken to Your servant—because I have a slow mouth and a heavy tongue." But, as He did with Moses' other doubts about why He was chosen to free the Hebrews, God said, "I will be with you." God called Moses, and God would give him the gevurah—the strength—to do what He asked him to do.

I believe God is calling many to be like Moses for this season. There is a transition that is happening. Just as God called Moses from being a shepherd of sheep to a shepherd of the people, I believe that many of us are going to be drawn into the real purpose and calling for which God created us. We've been faithful out in the desert with the sheep, and now, with new strength and the breakthrough to enter in, we, like Moses, can lead ourselves and others to breakthrough.

The Mishnaic sage Ben Zoma answers a question for us: "Who is *Gibbor*, the mighty one? He who subdues his evil inclinations." Proverbs 16:32 tells us, "He that is slow to anger is better than the mighty; and he that ruleth his spirit than he that taketh a city" (KJV). The sages and the Bible tell us we have the strength to overcome our inner urges and challenges, and when we do, it ultimately leads to purity in our life. Purity in Greek, *hagneía*, has a numerical value of eighty.

Paul counsels young Timothy to command and to be an example of purity (1 Timothy 4:12). The only way Timothy, with all the pressures of being a young pastor in a newly established church, could succeed is by setting aside the anxieties and challenges, and relying on God for strength. It's a strength that also makes us capable of shedding what is holding us back. In his commentary, F. B. Meyer wrote about this verse, saying, "There are infinite resources in God, which He is waiting to employ in human affairs, and of which we fail to make use."[5] Let's believe God's calling for us, and use the strength available to us, like Moses, to break through to personal freedom and lead others to freedom as well.

Yeshua/Jesus

Ultimately, we have the Lord and the strength of His might because we are in Messiah Yeshua. Remember this verse from Isaiah 9: "For to us a child is born, a son will be given to us, and the government will be upon His shoulder. His Name will be called [*Pele Yoetz*] Wonderful Counselor, [*El-gibbor*] Mighty God, [*Avi Ad*], My Father of Eternity, [*Sar shalom*] Prince of Peace" (v. 5). He is El Gibbor, The Mighty One,

---

5   F. B. Meyer, *Through the Bible Day by Day*, Published in 1914, Public Domain.

from the word *gevurah,* and we have His might because, at salvation, we are in Him. In Him, we are in part of what He is—mighty (Ephesians 2:1–10). Therefore, we can become mighty and strong, and since this is the decade of eighty, the decade of the mouth, we need to openly declare, "I am strong in the Lord and the strength of His might. I will overcome internal and external oppositions by God's power."

2

Eighty: Transcending Our Natural Limitations

EIGHTY IS ALSO the number of exceptional. To requote Psalm 90:10, "The span of our years is seventy—or with strength, eighty—yet at best they are trouble and sorrow. For they are soon gone, and we fly away." This psalm, attributed to Moses, reminds us that living until seventy is the ordinary, and living to eighty is going beyond the norm. God created the world in seven days; it is the completion of the physical world. The number eight is going beyond the natural order; it is the transcending of the natural order. This is why the Messiah died on the sixth day, was buried on the seventh day, and He rose from the dead on the eighth day. Eighty is the number of new beginnings, breakthrough, and the exceptional. It's the power to excel. So, in this decade of eighty, God wants us to move past the illusions of who we think we are to know the reality of who we are in Him.

KNOWING WHO WE ARE IN HIM

We are unique, and we can *break through* because we are in Yeshua. We can *excel* because we are in Him. We can *transcend* any natural limitations because we are in Him.

The Apostle Paul in Ephesians 1:7–10 tells us, "In Him we have redemption through His blood—the removal of trespasses—in keeping with the richness of His grace that He lavished on us. In all wisdom and insight, He made known to us the mystery of His will, in keeping with His good pleasure that He planned in Messiah. The plan of the fullness of times is to bring all things together in the Messiah—both things in heaven and things on earth, all in Him."

> It is in the Messiah Jesus that we have redemption, and it is through Him that we will have the strength to overcome the natural tendencies that hold us back from our breakthrough.

It is in the Messiah Jesus that we have redemption, and it is through Him that we will have the strength to overcome the natural tendencies that hold us back from our breakthrough.

We have been brought back from the dominion of darkness through the blood of the Messiah. Yeshua-Jesus redeems us, forgives us, and gives us the wisdom to know His will and way. We can live as His favored son or daughter because He loves us and wants us to break through the obstacles we face, to an extraordinary life.

Are you aware that you and I have been given the mind of Yeshua? When we live entirely in Him, we can think as He thinks and feel as He feels. We have this inheritance—not merely His character traits, but we also have access to His ability to make wise decisions and love others. We have this awesome ability, like little children, to grow in our relationship with Jesus and develop the mind of the Messiah. We can break through because He loves us, wants to help us, and gives us all we need through Him to live in the overflow.

KNOWING WE ARE A ROYAL PRIESTHOOD

Eighty is the power to excel. It is also connected to priesthood. The Hebrew word for *priesthood* is *Kehuna*, which has the numerical value of eighty. Interestingly, the Hebrew word is connected to big *kahuna*—which is the proto-Polynesian word for *priest*, which must have been taken from the Hebrew.

The Jewish people were called to be priestly people. This is the power of eighty, as the priesthood centered around eight and eighty (eight times ten, meaning a tremendous increase). For example, the high priest wore eight holy garments (*bigdei kodesh*). Also, prior to King David's changes in priestly divisions (1 Chronicles 24:3–5), there were eight priestly divisions. Exodus 19:5 tells us that Israel was to be a nation of priests. All Israel was called to be a royal priesthood. The power of eighty extends to the nation of Israel as a whole. Despite persecution and small numbers, Jews have excelled and pushed boundaries in spiritual business, academics, science, and the arts.

> God wants you to excel in both your identity and your destiny. Knowing you possess a royal identity and priestly calling is a critical experience that leads to more significant breakthroughs in your life.

This concept to excel extends to believers as well. Peter wrote in 1 Peter 2:9, "But you are a chosen people, a royal priesthood, a holy nation, a people for God's own possession, so that you may proclaim the praises of the One who called you out of darkness into His marvelous light." We have the power to change and excel when we remember who we are—in Him, a royal priesthood, and God's special possession. Max Lucado wrote:

> *Do you ever feel unnoticed? New clothes and styles may help for a while. But if you want permanent change, learn to see yourself as God sees you: "He has covered me with clothes of salvation and wrapped me with a coat of goodness, like a bridegroom dressed for his wedding, like a bride dressed in jewels" (Isa. 61:10).*
>
> *Does your self-esteem ever sag? When it does, remember what you are worth. "You were bought, not with*

something that ruins like gold or silver, but with the precious blood of Christ, who was like a pure and perfect lamb" (1 Pet. 1:18–19).[6]

God wants you to excel in both your identity and your destiny. Knowing you possess a royal identity and priestly calling is a critical experience that leads to more significant breakthroughs in your life. Identity is destiny, so the more you know who you are in Yeshua-Jesus, the more you will excel and experience a breakthrough in your destiny.

On the Gregorian calendar, we have entered into the year and the decade of 2020. This has a significant connection to the decade of the '80s on the Hebrew calendar. Greek as well as Hebrew is alphanumeric. In Greek, 2020 is the numeric value of the phrase "according to the order of Melchizedek" (Hebrews 7:17). In both Hebrew and Greek, this decade is connected to stepping into our priestly calling and identity.

As well, 2020 is the numeric value of the Greek word for *conformed (súmmorphos)*. Paul writes in Romans 8:29, "For those whom He foreknew He also predestined to be *conformed* to the image of His Son" (emphasis added). You will be robbed of your future and true identity if you allow yourself to be conformed to what the world, the flesh, and the

---

6   Max Lucado and Terri A. Gibbs, *Grace for the Moment: Inspirational Thoughts for Each Day of the Year* (Nashville, TN: J. Countryman, 2000), 17.

Enemy have to say about you (or other people). You must conform to transform into the image of the Son, who is both a royal Son and High Priest. You are called to be both in Him.

It's the decade of breakthrough. It's the decade of transformation. Since it is the decade of the mouth, we need to declare, "I will excel. I am not ordinary. I am extraordinary. I can break through to an exceptional life in Yeshua-Jesus!"

BUILDING ON A SOLID FOUNDATION

Eighty is the number of the *yesod*. In Hebrew, *yesod* means "foundation" and has a numerical value of eighty. The decade of 5780 is a foundational decade, and this is a foundational season. God is establishing new foundations in our lives. We need to remember the natural and the spiritual go hand in hand. If we are going to break through natural limitations, there are new spiritual foundations we need to establish. Proverbs 10:25 reminds us, "When the whirlwind passes, the wicked are no more, but the foundation [yesod] of the righteous is everlasting."

Joseph (Genesis 37–50) is associated with foundations. He was thirty years old when he became viceroy of Egypt. He held the position for eighty years. Joseph brought order everywhere he went. The order he brought led to alignment, and that alignment led to blessing. He put Potiphar's house in order. He put the prison in order. He put the Egyptian palace in order. When he put these things in order, they came into alignment, and the result was multiplication and blessing as he laid the foundation for the Hebrews' future in Israel.

God wants to bring new order to our lives and to our nation. God wants to remove the chaos. The first thing God did at creation was to create *seder* (order). Nothing can exist until He brings order out of chaos. God wants to bring order into your life to firm up a shaky foundation or establish a new foundation so that alignment and blessing can come in unprecedented ways. Your foundation is directly connected to eighty (breakthrough) and transcending natural limitations.

Joseph overcame incredible temptation (Genesis 39:6–23). Temptation is something we must grapple with in our lives. How did Joseph transcend what many would call "natural" temptations? He trusted God. He understood that true blessing comes from walking with God and does not have anything to do with circumstances. His understanding of his own times empowered him to *not* do certain things.

Joseph resisted and retained his integrity. Just as the Apostle Paul advised Timothy about purity, which in Greek is eighty. Paul wrote, "Let no one look down on your youthfulness, but become an example of the faithful—in speech, in conduct, in love, in faithfulness, and in purity" (1 Timothy 4:12). Paul is exhorting Timothy to be like Joseph. Before any temptation came Joseph's way, he had already built a solid personal foundation (yesod) of trusting God and knowing, deep in his heart, that God would do something mighty in his life. Joseph transcended those circumstances by believing the words Solomon would later write in Proverbs 10:25—that a foundation of righteousness is everlasting.

The hymn "How Firm a Foundation" was first published in 1787 in a hymnbook edited by John Rippon titled *A Selection of Hymns from the Best Authors*. Its beautiful lyrics exalting the Word of God have made it one of America's best-loved hymns. Surprisingly, the name of the author behind this classic hymn is a mystery. In the hymnbook, it was attributed only to "K—." This is thought by many to be a reference to Robert Keene, who was a friend of John Rippon and the leader of music at the Carter Lane Baptist Church in London when Rippon was the pastor. Even so, the true identity of the author remains a mystery.

Despite the anonymity of its origin, for over 230 years "How Firm a Foundation" has brought comfort and encouragement to countless believers. It was sung at the death bed of President Andrew Jackson and at the funerals of Robert E. Lee and Theodore Roosevelt."[7]

This song's lyrics remind us of the importance of building a firm foundation, on Yeshua-Jesus, if we want to transcend our natural limitations and break through. Part of the lyric says this:

---

7 "Hymn Story: How Firm a Foundation," *Reasonable Theology*, https://reasonabletheology.org/hymn-story-how-firm-a-foundation/.

How firm a foundation, ye saints of the Lord,
is laid for your faith in His excellent Word!
What more can He say than to you He hath said,
who unto the Savior for refuge have fled?

In every condition, in sickness, in health,
in poverty's vale, or abounding in wealth,
at home and abroad, on the land, on the sea,
as days may demand, shall thy strength ever be.

Like Joseph, we need a firm foundation of trust in God, standing on His strength to pull us through every circumstance, and every natural tendency that wants to keep us in the bondage of our past, our pain, and our circumstances.

We are living in the decade of the mouth. Let's declare that we are trusting God to help us build a rock-solid foundation.

3

Understanding the Significance of the Last Decade

WE CAN'T FULLY understand breakthrough in this decade of 5780 without fully understanding the significance of the prior decade, 5770. The previous decade was the decade of the *ayin*. The letter *ayin* is the sixteenth letter of the Hebrew alphabet. The word *ayin* means "eye, to see," and has a numeric value of seventy. Throughout this past decade Jews have

ayin

been reminded of Psalm 36:10, "For with You is the fountain of life—in Your light we see light." Similarly, David wrote in Psalm 27:13, "Surely I trust that I will see the goodness of ADONAI in the land of the living." The *ayin* was a reminder to see things with God's perspective.

This new decade is the decade of the mouth, while the previous decade was the decade of the eye.

THE GOOD EYE AND THE BAD EYE

The previous decade involved learning to see differently. Because until we learn to see differently, we will never be different. The ayin is often described as having two eyes, and we have two eyes. Symbolically, two eyes represent actions or choices of the will—one eye is known as the good eye and one is known as the bad, or evil, eye. Yeshua-Jesus talks about this in Matthew 6:22–23 when He says, "The eye is the lamp of the body; so then if your eye is clear, your whole body will be full of light. But if your eye is bad, your whole body will be full of darkness. If then the light that is in you is darkness, how great is the darkness!" (NASB).

> Looking at the world through the good eye is vital to breakthrough. The good eye sees the blessing, abundant and hopeful life, and good in all people, circumstances, and situations.

In these two verses, Yeshua-Jesus is speaking about the good eye and the bad eye. What is the bad eye? It is the pessimistic eye. It is the cynical eye. The bad eye is always the eye that lets us see the cloud instead of the silver lining. To the degree that we see through the bad eye, we will remain stuck in Egypt (confinement) and miss the breakthrough. Some rabbis believe that as many as one-third of the Hebrew population died during the ninth plague, the plague of darkness (Exodus 10:21–29). They could not see literally or spiritually, and they died in Egypt. They preferred Egypt instead of flee-ing bondage and moving to the Promised Land with Moses.

Looking at the world through the good eye is vital to breakthrough. The good eye sees the blessing, abundant and hopeful life, and good in all people, circumstances, and sit-uations. The eye is physically connected to the brain, but the good eye and bad eye is a function of the mind (interpret-ing what the physical eyes and ears take in). How we decide to see the world determines how we will process the experi-ences that we have. That's why two people (or twelve spies, as we'll learn below) can look at the same event and come to very different conclusions and understandings.

Breakthrough begins with thinking and seeing with our good eye. The decade of the eye (ayin) must precede the de-cade of the mouth (peh) because we always have to see with the good eye before we can speak fittingly. Usually, seeing should precede speaking.

THE TWELVE SPIES

We find an excellent example of seeing and speaking after Israel fled from Egypt. Moses sent twelve spies into Canaan, the Promised Land, to spy it out (Numbers 13–14). Ten of the spies could only see the problems and pitfalls in Canaan and returned to Israel's camp speaking about everything that was wrong with the Promised Land. Only two spies could see the good.

Twelve spies returned from the mission, and ten of them gave an unfavorable report. Those ten allowed their bad eye to prevail. They said, "The land is good. It flows with milk and honey. It's amazing. Look at the enormous fruit we carried back. It was excellent, *but* . . ."

Friends, your big *buts* will always get you into trouble. Why do we want to insert our big *buts* into God's plans for us? *But* is the most dangerous word we can say when God shows us something that we assume He can't handle because we can only see it through our bad eye.

He told those spies they would possess the land, yet they didn't believe Him. Your big *buts* will rob you of your breakthrough and life in the overflow. Every one of us has a *but* that keeps us from transformation and breakthrough.

In this story, the ten spies let fear keep them from living the life God intended to give them. They were afraid of the giants and fortified cities. Their lousy eyesight led to wrong thinking, which led to negative speaking, which undermined the children of Israel's faith, causing that generation of Israelites to wander in the desert for forty years, where they died. Their bad eye caused them to bad-mouth the Promised Land and even God and His promises.

We can't understand the decade of the mouth until we understand the decade of the eyes. The eyes and mouth are connected. The two spies who gave a favorable report, Joshua and Caleb, had a different spirit. They looked at the "obstacles" in the Promised Land through their hope-filled, faith-filled good eye because they had their eyes on God. They said, "There are giants in the land—so what? There are fortified cities—so what? Don't listen to the bad report; listen to God's promises. Let's go up and let God give us the breakthrough. God will empower us to break through."

But is the most dangerous word we can say when God shows us something that we assume He can't handle because we can only see it through our bad eye.

The Apostle John wrote, "You are from God, children, and you have overcome them, because greater is He who is in you than he who is in the world." We can have a breakthrough when we move in God's time as we see with our good eye. There's an anointing that moves us through whatever He's called us to do. If we stare with our bad eye at the Enemy too long, we can think ourselves out of victory and breakthrough. The ten spies spent too much time talking about the problems, while Joshua and Caleb spoke about how God would work out (or transcend) any obstacle they faced.

Unfortunately, the Hebrews followed their bad eye and not their good eye. Joshua and Caleb had faith. They were the only two adults who did not die in the wilderness, because they believed. Years later, Caleb, at eighty-five years old, told Joshua, "I want to go up and take Hebron." What's impressive about that? It was the place of the giants. At eighty-five years old, Caleb asked for the toughest assignment. The word *peh* is spelled *peh heh*. Peh is eighty, and heh is five. Caleb used his mouth (eighty-five) to ask for the area of Canaan that was the most challenging because it involved defeating giants. His mouth was greater than these monstrous men he had to face to gain his inheritance. He used his mouth, and he chose to see through his good eye.

We can learn so much from Caleb. He teaches us that we will never break through if we don't think we are able. Do we honestly believe Romans 8:31? Do we believe as Paul wrote, "What then shall we say in view of these things? If God is for us, who can be against us?"

Who can be against us? Circumstances, disease, exhaustion, work, and fears to name a few. Paul tells us that God is for us. If we want a breakthrough, we need to know who we are in the Messiah, and we need to look at everything through the good eye. Then we can step out like Caleb, trusting God because we know what He is capable of doing for us and through us.

Our sight either leads to "breakthrough thinking" or wrong "stinking thinking" that ultimately affects what comes out of our mouths. And our mouths are as important—if not more so—to a breakthrough than our eyes are.

4

The Power of Peh: The Mouth Is Key to Breakthrough

OUR MOUTHS ARE as important as our eyes for breakthrough.

When we look at the written letter *peh*, there's a bet hidden within it. *Bet* means "to build" but it also means "house." It symbolizes God creating a home in this world. The peh represents the mouth and, by extension, "word" and "expression." Psalm 33:6 says, "By ADONAI's word were the heavens made, and all their host by the breath of His mouth."

The peh is the mouth. The fifth letter of the Hebrew alphabet, heh, is the letter of the divine breath. The Talmud (*Menachot* 29b) says that the "breath of His mouth" refers to the sound of the letter *heh*—the outbreathing of Spirit. It is the breath that comes from the

heh

mouth that creates the world in which we live, the bet. There is a spiritual significance—there is power in the mouth. The

49

mouth of God created the world, and our mouth creates our world. Our words bring life, and our words create our world.

THE POWER OF AGREEMENT

So why is it so significant for the letter *bet* to be inside the letter *peh*? The letter *bet* has the numeric value of two—the number two is inside the Hebrew letter for "mouth." The number two points to the power of agreement, which is key to breakthrough. By two or more, a matter is established. By the spoken declaration of the mouth, a testimony is established. The word *testimony* comes from the word *od*, which means "again."

When it comes to God's testimony, it's not something that happened in the past; it's something He wants to do again and again. Subsequently, coming into agreement with God and His promises for our life is an essential part of any breakthrough we experience. Remember the spies? Ten disagreed, and only the two who agreed went on to take the Promised Land. There was agreement and breakthrough because of the testimony of the two.

In Matthew 18:19–20, Yeshua-Jesus tells us, "Again, truly I tell you that if two of you on earth agree about anything they ask for, it will be done for them by my Father in heaven. For where two or three gather in my name, there am I with them" (NIV). Why did He say if *two* ask? It's the power of agreement. It's agreement that establishes a testimony that then becomes legally binding. Of course, the two in agreement have to be in agreement with God's Word, His promises, and His plans. We need to see what God sees. We need to declare those promises in agreement with God (that is one) and agreement with others (that is two) to call forth things that are not, as if they were.

The problem is when we speak negatively about someone or about ourselves, a testimony is also established. God speaks good, but the accuser of the brethren is always speaking for bad. So, when we speak bad, we are agreeing with the accuser and bringing a legal accusation against someone. When we speak evil about someone, we are bearing testimony against an individual, which then makes it a legal issue. So use your mouth to agree for good. See the good. Call forth the good in agreement and declaration during this season in which it is crucial to do so.

> Coming into agreement with God and His promises for our life is an essential part of any breakthrough we experience. Remember the spies? Ten disagreed, and only the two who agreed went on to take the Promised Land. There was agreement and breakthrough because of the testimony of the two.

SPEAKING OFTEN PRECEDES SEEING

In the world, seeing is believing. The eyes see and the mouth speaks—this is what bearing witness and giving testimony are based upon. But this is not how the Kingdom works. Most of the time, we are conditioned by the natural world that we must see something before we can speak about it.

However, in the Kingdom, speaking often proceeds seeing. When Yeshua appeared to the disciples after His resurrection, He said, "Blessed are the ones who have not seen and yet have believed." He's saying that the people who are blessed are those who, even though their eyes have not seen Yeshua-Jesus, their mouths profess faith.

> If you want the kind of breakthrough I'm talking about, you must understand that seeing is not believing, but believing is seeing. This kind of faith is kingdom faith. This kingdom-focused faith is the kind of faith that moves mountains.

Writer, teacher, and twentieth-century pastor Andrew Murray put it this way: "Faith adheres simply to what God says. The unbelief that would see shall not see; the faith that will not see, but has enough in God, shall see the glory of God."[8] In the Kingdom, speaking is believing.

Later in this book, we will spend more time with Israel's twelve spies. Ten came back and based their decision on what they saw in the natural, but Joshua and Caleb based their decision on the peh—not on what they saw, but on what God's

---

8 Andrew Murray, *The New Life: Words of God for Young Disciples of Christ* (New York: Hurst & Company, 1891), 100.

peh had to say. They believed God's declared promise to the Israelites to give them the land.

The creation account gives us another example. Genesis 1:3–4 says, "Then God said, 'Let there be light!' And there was light. God saw that the light was good. So God distinguished the light from darkness." Notice that God speaks, then He sees that it is good. God calls the good into being before He sees the light. We need to be like God—we must speak the good before we see the good.

If you want the kind of breakthrough I'm talking about, you must understand that seeing is not believing, but believing is seeing. This kind of faith is Kingdom faith. This Kingdom-focused faith is the kind of faith that moves mountains. Yes, there are giants, but what does God's peh say? What are His promises we can believe without seeing? For Joshua and Caleb, seeing the land was simply a formality. These two men already believed the promise that proceeded from the peh of God.

Peh faith is powerful.

Peh faith is creation faith—it releases the Lord's creative power and potential in you.

Peh faith is the type of faith that calls forth things that are not as if they were. Paul writes in Romans 4:16–22 (TPT, emphasis mine):

> *The promise depends on faith so that it can be experienced as a grace-gift, and now it extends to all the descendants*

of Abraham. *This promise is not only meant for those who obey the law, but also to those who enter into the faith of Abraham, the father of us all. . . .*

*He is our example and father, for in God's presence he believed that God can raise the dead **and call into being things that don't even exist yet.***

***Against all odds, when it looked hopeless,** Abraham believed the promise and expected God to fulfill it. He took God at his word, and as a result he became the father of many nations. God's declaration over him came to pass:*

> In the moments of crushing pain, in the moments of our garden of Gethsemane, when we feel like we are being pressed and shaken, we can't trust our eyes. We can't live by what we see. In these difficult circumstances, the eyes are not going to be the key to breakthrough, because the pain blurs our vision.

"Your descendants will be so many

that they will be impossible to count!"

In spite of being nearly one hundred years old when the promise of having a son was made, his faith was so strong that it could not be undermined by the fact that he and Sarah were incapable of conceiving a child. He never stopped believing God's promise, for he was made *strong in his faith to father a child. **And because he was mighty in faith and convinced that God had all the power needed to fulfill his promises, Abraham glorified God!***

So now you can see why Abraham's faith was credited to his account as righteousness before God.

Abraham believed before he saw. Even though it looked hopeless for him to have descendants, he believed in the peh God. He knew God's promise was already fulfilled even without seeing his wife pregnant, and also with the impossibility of conceiving a child at age ninety. Abraham's faith was powerful, and it was rewarded with a son, Isaac.

True faith—creation faith—comes not by seeing. If the Lord says it, we need to believe it. We don't need additional evidence. We should believe because He declared it.

PAIN AND FEAR BLURS OUR VISION

We need to understand that pain blurs our vision. Our minds become overwhelmed by the negative. There are times when our eyes can't see God's good because we are hurt, and when we are hurt, our vision becomes distorted. Our pain prevents us from accurately seeing, thinking, and feeling. In the moments of crushing pain, in the moments of our garden of Gethsemane, when we feel like we are being pressed and shaken, we can't trust our eyes. We can't live by what we see. In these difficult circumstances, the eyes are not going to be the key to breakthrough, because the pain blurs our vision.

In those pressing moments, the mouth is going to be the key to our breakthrough. What do I mean by that? In those challenging moments, our eyes must submit to our mouths. Sometimes, the power of peh is more significant than the power of our eyes (ayin).

King David wrote in Psalm 92:2, "To declare Your lovingkindness in the morning and your faithfulness by night" (NASB). Why does he write this? He knew that when we have God's lovingkindness, His love is like light. Everything is shining and happy. Everything is great. We declare love in the morning, but why do we declare His faithfulness at night? Because it's when we are hurt that we often can't see God's hand due to the darkness surrounding us. Therefore, even when we can't see God's loving hand, we declare that He is faithful. Even when we can't see the hand of God, we have to trust the heart of God by proclaiming the promises and faithfulness of God. At those moments, we say, "Lord, even when I can't see your hand, I am going to declare the heart of God and Your promises for my life."

What God has done in the past gives us assurance of what He will do for us in the present. That's when the mouth becomes a critical key to breakthrough. In this year of the peh, we need to proclaim the power of God's promises, what He has done for us, and the truth of His Word. When pain blurs our vision, the mouth is the key to breakthrough in every area of life.

There are also times when fear gets in the way of our faith. Fear discourages us and it distorts God's purposes and plans for us. Fear gets in the way of our breakthrough. The Lord spoke to the prophet Isaiah and said, "Fear not, for I am with you, be not dismayed, for I am your God. I will strengthen you. Surely I will help you. I will uphold you with My righteous right hand." There are so many promises in this verse.

THE POWER OF BREAKTHROUGH PRAISE

The power of peh also involves breakthrough praise. We sometimes go through worship with a "whatever" attitude. That's not breakthrough praise. Breakthrough praise changes the atmosphere. It deeply stirs our emotions.

I knew a man who had terminal cancer. His doctors told him there was nothing they could do for him and he only had several months to live. After hearing the doctor's words, he decided he wasn't going to ask anyone for more prayer for healing. He felt what God put on his heart was to praise Him. Instead of praying for healing, he merely praised God for His goodness and faithfulness. My friend praised God for his family, his friends, and his salvation. He praised everything. In this man's praise, God broke through and healed him.

There is breakthrough praise, and even if God doesn't heal us like He did my friend, praising God still can lead to a deeper breakthrough within us. Songwriter and worship leader Darlene Zschech wrote, "If you can casually meander through worship, then I would dare to say that maybe, just maybe, you have not entered into true worship at all. We need Jesus-centered, Holy Spirit–filled, passionately led worship. Because when God comes close, everything changes. . . . When we worship, thanksgiving is our entry point, joy is our strength, and breakthrough is our inheritance."[9]

It's time to open our mouths in praise. It's time to be like David and say:

> *I will exalt you, my God the King;*
>
> *I will praise your name for ever and ever.*
>
> *Every day I will praise you*
>
> *and extol your name for ever and ever.*
>
> *Great is the LORD and most worthy of praise;*
>
> *his greatness no one can fathom.*
>
> *(Psalm 145:1–3, NIV)*

David knew the power of breakthrough praise. He didn't praise God one day a week; he worshiped Him every day,

---

9 Darlene Zschech, *Worship Changes Everything: Experiencing God's Presence in Every Moment of Life* (Minneapolis, MN: Bethany House Publishers, 2016), Kindle Edition.

and forever and ever. That's breakthrough praise that has the power to transform our lives to be what God wants for us.

David, as well as Yeshua-Jesus, traces his lineage back to Perez, the son of Judah and Tamar. *Perez* means "breakthrough," and his father's name *Judah* means "praise." In other words, breakthroughs are born of praise. David and Yeshua-Jesus, the Son of David, lived a life of praise that empowered them to breakthrough seemingly impossible barriers and obstacles. A life of praise gives you the power to defeat your Goliaths.

THE POWER OF BREAKTHROUGH PRAYER

"Lord, teach us to pray." Yes, to pray. This is what we need to be taught. Though in its beginnings prayer is so simple that the feeble child can pray, yet it is at the same time the highest and holiest work to which man can rise. It is fellowship with the Unseen and Most Holy One. The powers of the eternal world have been placed at its disposal. It is the very essence of true religion, the channel of all blessings, the secret of power and life.[10]

Not only breakthrough praise, but also breakthrough prayer leads to transformation, breakthrough, and blessing.

---

10 Andrew Murray, *Lord, Teach Us to Pray* (Philadelphia: Henry Altemus, 1896), 6–7.

God has been talking to me about breakthrough prayer. Sometimes we offer up these wishy-washy prayers. We do our duty to send a few prayers up to heaven. We need to stop focusing on what we're supposed to do in prayer. Breakthrough prayer is not a to-do list item we casually check off. We should come to prayer frequently, with our hearts open to fellowship and conversation with "the Unseen and Most Holy One."

Much like breakthrough praise, breakthrough prayer needs to be intentional and from our heart. We can't pray routine prayers that only serve to treat God like some kind of cosmic Coke machine, ready to serve our every whim. Breakthrough prayers are genuine, expectant, and free of doubt. These prayers are spoken with a sincere knowledge of the power of God, with a faith that believes that God will work out all things for our good according to His Word. When we pray like that, we can experience a breakthrough.

> We can't pray routine prayers that only serve to treat God like some kind of cosmic Coke machine, ready to serve our every whim. Breakthrough prayers are genuine, expectant, and free of doubt. These prayers are spoken with a sincere knowledge of the power of God, with a faith that believes that God will work out all things for our good according to His Word.

Yeshua-Jesus gives us some profound insight in Matthew 7:7–11 when He says:

> *"Ask, and it shall be given to you. Seek, and you shall find. Knock, and it shall be opened to you. For everyone who asks receives, and the one who seeks finds, and to the one who knocks it shall be opened.*
>
> *"For what man among you, when his son asks him for bread, will give him a stone? Or when he asks for a fish, will give him a snake? If you then, being evil, know how to give good gifts to your children, how much more will your Father in heaven give good things to those who ask Him!"*

To experience the power of breakthrough prayer, we should ask specifically for the breakthrough we need. We also need to live as people who pray about everything, realizing that if we ask God for a breakthrough into a new and different life, He will not give us anything that will harm us or lead us away from Him. Even if God gives us something different from what we prayed for, we need to trust that what He has given us is far better than whatever we requested.

Do we trust God enough to ask for that specific breakthrough? Let's not allow the Egypt mentality to confine us. In the decade of the peh, we can declare, "I am unafraid to ask God for my breakthrough."

5

The Promises of Breakthrough

WHEN I THINK of breakthrough, one of the leading biblical people I think of is Jacob. For most of his life, Jacob tried to get the breakthrough and blessing in his strength. Jacob, dressed like his older brother Esau, tricked his father and received the blessing of the firstborn son. Then he fled from his father's house, thinking Esau was going to kill him for his trickery. Jacob was scared.

He came to a particular place to sleep that night and saw a ladder (*Sulam Ya'akov*) extending to heaven (Genesis 28:12). Jacob had an encounter with an angel and, surprisingly, the Lord was standing on the top of the ladder. He named that particular place *Beth-El*, the house of God, and God blessed him there, saying, "Your seed will be as the dust of the land and burst forth to the west and to the east and to the north and to the south" (Genesis 28:14). The phrase *burst forth* is *pârats*, or "breakthrough," in Hebrew. God blessed Jacob with a breakthrough.

We need to note that Jacob had the *promise* of a breakthrough, but he didn't have the *experience* of a breakthrough.

Jacob left Beth-El and moved on to live with his Uncle Laban, who continually tried to cheat him. After Jacob agreed to work for seven years in order to marry his daughter Rachel, Laban switched one daughter for another on the wedding night, and Jacob ended up working for fourteen years (and having two wives!). Then Laban went on to change the wages he pledged to pay Jacob, proposing some shady deals with sheep.

> Make this declaration:
> No one will rob me of
> my breakthrough and
> my blessing.

Despite all of this, the Scriptures tell us that "the man [Jacob] grew exceedingly prosperous" (Genesis 30:43). The word for *exceedingly prosperous* is again *pârats*, or "breakthrough." He "had numerous flocks along with male and female servants, camels and donkeys." Jacob was prosperous. He had a breakthrough in spite of Laban's deception. Laban was trying to cheat Jacob any way he could, but God had promised Jacob a breakthrough.

Here's the point: no one can rob you of your breakthrough. People can lie to you, they can try to cheat you, and they can try to steal from you. It doesn't make a difference if God promised you a breakthrough. No one can rob you of your breakthrough, except one person—yourself. If you honor God and follow Him, your breakthrough will come.

People, like Laban, can scheme all they want against you, but they won't be able to hold you back when a breakthrough is what God has promised.

Make this declaration: No one will rob me of my breakthrough and my blessing.

At this point in his life, however, Jacob still had not *experienced* the breakthrough. God told him to return home, where he must face Esau, whom he presumed wanted to kill him. In an effort to defend himself, Jacob divided the camps, but ultimately endured a sleepless night because he was nervous.

An angel came and wrestled with him, and the encounter transformed Jacob; he was transformed from Jacob into Israel: "Then He said to him, 'What is your name?' 'Jacob,' he said. Then He said, 'Your name will no longer be Jacob, but rather Israel, for you have struggled with God and with men, and you have overcome'" (Genesis 32:28–29).

What does it mean for Jacob to wrestle with the Lord? Hosea 12:4–5 has the answer. The prophet wrote, "In the womb he grasped his brother's heel, and in his vigor he strove with God. Yes, he wrestled with an angel and won; he wept and sought his favor. At Bethel he will find us, and there He will speak with us." Jacob wept and made supplication (appeal) to God. His wrestling encounter with God is a powerful and mysterious example of breakthrough prayer. In order to *experience* breakthrough, sometimes we have to wrestle with God.

Jacob sought the Lord. Psalm 24:4–6 says, "One with clean hands and a pure heart, who has not lifted his soul in vain, nor sworn deceitfully. He will receive a blessing from ADONAI, righteousness from God his salvation. Such is the generation seeking Him, seeking Your face, even Jacob! *Selah.*" The word for face is *pânîym*, or *pâneh*, in Hebrew. Both words begin with peh. In the decade of the peh, if you want to experience a breakthrough, it's time to seek God's face (pânîym).

6

The Mouth (Peh) Is
Key to Redemption

BELIEVE THIS IS a decade and a season that God wants to lead us into and prepare us for a breakthrough. When I think about breakthrough, the story of Israel's redemption from Egypt is one of the most compelling images I find in all of Scripture. Egypt. *Egypt* in Hebrew is *Mitzrayim*, which literally means "a place of confinement or restriction." The word comes from the Hebrew word *tzar*, as in *min hametzer* used in Psalm 118:5: "Out of a *tight place* I called on ADONAI—ADONAI answered me with a spacious place" (emphasis added). Egypt is a place of confinement and restriction. It's a place of being boxed in and limited.

The decade of 5780 is the decade of the peh with an opportunity for breakthrough prayer, breakthrough praise, breakthrough declaration, and breakthrough agreement. The peh is also connected to redemption—out of our Egypt. It's time for us to come out of Egypt and the confinement that keeps us from God's redeeming breakthrough.

The word *peh* is connected to *pidyon*, the Hebrew word for redemption, which begins with the letter *peh*. Psalm 49:6–9 is attributed to the sons of Korah, who rebelled against Moses and Aaron. Consequently, Korah, his followers, and their families and possessions were swallowed by the ground in judgment from God. However, a few of his surviving descendants wrote these words:

> *Why should I fear in evil days?*
>
> *when the iniquity of my deceivers*
>   *surrounds me?*
>
> *Or those trusting in their wealth,*
>
> *boasting about their great riches?*
>
> *No man can redeem his brother,*
>
> *or give to God a ransom for him.*
>
> *For the redemption of a soul is costly—*
>
> *so, one should stop trying forever.*

In this psalm, *pidyon* is the word for redemption. It refers to a price that must be paid to redeem or rescue someone. It speaks of deliverance. Peh and this decade of 5780 are connected to redemption.

Pharaoh enslaved the Israelites. His title begins with peh. His rationale to oppress Israel—"the Israelites are multiplying, and if we're at war, they will join our enemies"—starts with the letter *peh*. *Lest* in Hebrew is *Pên* (Exodus 1:10) and begins with the letter *peh*. Moses was eighty years old when he led the Israelites out of Israel. As we mentioned earlier, the number eighty is the letter *peh*. Passover in Hebrew is *Pesach*, and it begins with the letter *peh*. The redemption from Egypt is all about the peh.

God multiplies the Hebrews in Egypt, and then Pharaoh afflicts them. Exodus 1:12 tells us that the more Pharaoh oppressed the Israelites, "the more they multiplied and the more they spread out" (NASB). The Hebrew word for *spread out* is *yif-rotz*, from the Hebrew root *paratz,* which means "breakthrough." The more Pharaoh and the Egyptians afflicted the Jews, the more they would break forth and spread out. Here's a critical point—no one can rob you of your breakthrough. God can use pain and persecution to bring about multiplication and breakthrough expansion.

Pharaoh was unhappy with the Hebrews' growth, and in the same way the world, the flesh, and the Enemy will oppose our spiritual growth and breakthrough. The more you break through, the more people will try to break you. People will want to break you when they see your breakthrough because it exposes their insecurity and awakens their jealousy. It's what Pharaoh realized when he witnessed the blessing of the Jewish people.

We need to recognize that there is a critical difference between being broken down (as Pharaoh tried to do) and holy brokenness (allowing the Lord to break us). Our brokenness is key to our breakthrough. God will break us before He gives us the breakthrough.

That was Jacob's experience before he had the ultimate breakthrough. He wrestled with the Lord and walked away with a limp. We shouldn't trust a leader who doesn't walk with a limp. We shouldn't trust a leader who hasn't experienced brokenness. Unbroken people are dangerous. Brokenness by God's hand is good. It's radically different than Pharaoh's violent insecurity; it leads to our blessing.

Too many people give up right before the breakthrough. In Exodus 5, Moses returned to Egypt in order to bring the breakthrough, and things got worse. Author and speaker Joyce Meyer wrote, "Instead of dwelling on our difficulties, we need to focus more on the fact that God is for us and His power is at work in us. Often, we give up too quickly, saying, 'this is too hard' or 'this is taking too long.' We must stop looking at situations. We need to say, 'I don't care whether there seems to be a way or not, Jesus is the Way.'"[11] Don't stop before you see your breakthrough. Trust that God is working even if situations or circumstances get harder.

We examined the word *peres*[12] earlier. It means to burst through the box, the confinement, and the limitations, and, like other words we've discussed in this section, it starts with the letter *peh*. Rather than constricting, peres is about expanding. It defines a life that is not being limited; it's excelling and being expansive. So don't allow yourself to be kept in the box. Don't let yourself be a slave in your own Egypt. You are redeemed. You need to focus on the Lord. You don't need to remain in Egypt. God wants you to break through.

Redemption is about the peh. All our trials and afflictions will lead to our breakthrough multiplication. The more Pharaoh afflicted the Israelites, the more they multiplied and grew. God promises us breakthrough. The Lord is our redeemer, and He will take us out of Egypt.

INNER AND OUTER BREAKTHROUGH

The peh is synonymous with Egypt and also with Moses. Moses was eighty years (peh) old when God called him. God told Moses to use his peh, his mouth, to speak to Pharaoh and

---

11 Joyce Meyer, *Never Give Up! Relentless Determination to Overcome Life's Challenges* (New York: FaithWords/Hachette Book Group, 2008), Kindle Edition.

12 This word can be spelled either *perez* or *peres*.

lead the Exodus, the Pesach. God talked to Moses like no other prophet. He spoke peh to peh, mouth to mouth. Moses didn't want to leave Midian. He told God he had a problem with his peh, his mouth. God asked him, "Who made your peh?"

> God was telling Moses, "Taking off your shoes is symbolic of removing those things that are locking you out of your breakthrough and receiving the blessing."

Moses needed to have an inner breakthrough before he could have an outer breakthrough—and so do we. Everyone wants a breakthrough, but it has to happen *in* us before it can happen *to* us.

God told Moses to take off his shoes because he was standing on "holy ground" (Exodus 3:5). Why did Moses have to take off his shoes? Our feet are the most sensitive part of our body, having more nerve endings per square inch than anywhere else in the body. Nerves are constantly sensing characteristics of the surface underfoot.[13] That's why we wear shoes—to create a barrier between us and the ground.

God commanded Moses to take off his shoes because anything that separates us from the most profound connection to God and His holiness has to be stripped away. God wanted a complete relationship with Moses. God was saying, "Moses, be here. Be completely connected to me—to my

13 "Why Do Our Feet Have so Many Nerve Endings if We Are Constantly Stepping on Them?" *Reference*, https://www.reference.com/science/feet-many-nerve-endings-constantly-stepping-f6d36b17817c3bb8.

presence, to my holiness. Anything that separates you has to be removed."

In Hebrew, the word for shoes (na'al) is connected to the word for lock (man'ûl). The two words come from the same root. God was telling Moses, "Taking off your shoes is symbolic of removing those things that are locking you out of your breakthrough and receiving the blessing." He was saying, "Unlock whatever is locking you up on the inside, and whatever is creating that disconnection between you and my promises. Moses, you have to take off your shoes in order to unlock all the inner barriers."

Some of us have inner barriers—inner fears like Moses had—and they're keeping us locked in the box. Part of the key to unlocking our box is taking off our shoes and allowing ourselves to be exposed, allowing ourselves to be wholly connected. We must remove anything that is creating separation between us and God (and all that He has for us).

Moses didn't think he could handle the assignment. He didn't think he had the mouth (peh); he needed signs. And what was the first sign? God told him to take his staff and throw it down, and it became a snake (Exodus 4:2–5). A snake is symbolic of Satan, but it was also a symbol of Pharaoh (as was the crocodile). God told Moses, "Take the snake by the tail—take your fear by the tail. The person that you fear, Pharaoh, thinks he's a crocodile in the Nile, but he's only a snake, and guess what? You just picked him up. Moses, you've nothing to fear."

Friends, God has the authority to turn our snake (our fears) into a staff. We can take our fear by the tail.

PROPHETIC VISION LEADS TO BREAKTHROUGH

God's vision is another key to the breakthrough. You need to see who you are (your identity in Christ) as well as His purpose, calling, and mission for your life from the divine perspective.

Moses needed to have a personal breakthrough before He could help Israel break forth and break out of slavery. Moses needed to have his identity transformed. And when His identity was transformed, so was his destiny. Often, it's our destiny that transforms our identity. Moses went from being a shepherd of sheep to a shepherd of Israel. That was God's prophetic vision for him.

The disciples experienced a similar transformation going from fishermen to fishers of men. God used who the disciples were and where they came from to make them into what they were destined to be.

Twelve men answered Yeshua-Jesus' call (John 14:16). They were ordinary, Jewish working-class individuals. They were common men, not executives or leaders within the temple. They gave up everything to follow Yeshua-Jesus. He had a vision for them to make disciples of all nations. With this vision, these common men turned the world upside down. Yeshua's vision became their passion and the driving force that enabled them to endure hardship, torture, and excruciating deaths.

First Samuel 3:1 says, "Now the boy Samuel was in the service of ADONAI under Eli. In those days the word of ADONAI was rare—there were no visions breaking through." The phrase *no open vision* literally means no breakthrough vision. Breakthrough vision involves the peh, the mouth. God spoke to Moses face-to-face—mouth to mouth.

Song of Solomon opens by saying, "Let him kiss me with the kisses of his mouth!" (Song of Solomon 1:2). Kissing, in this context, is understood as God revealing deep intimate truth and revelation to His beloved. Mouth to mouth is the most intimate communication we can have with God. It's the type of breakthrough vision and revelation that Moses and the Messiah Yeshua-Jesus received.

In the New Testament, Yeshua-Jesus promises an amazing level of intimacy and mouth-to-mouth breakthrough vision when He states, "My sheep hear My voice" (John 10:27). A key to breakthrough is learning to listen to the Lord. God wants to communicate with us by His Word and Spirit. We must listen and obey like Moses to experience breakthrough.

7

Breakthrough Healing and Redemption

N OT ONLY IS it a time of redemption, of coming out of Egypt, but the letter *peh* is also associated with healing. The Hebrew word *rapha* means "to heal." Three letters make up the word: the first is the *resh*, the middle is  peh, and the last is heh. Notice the middle letter of the word for healing is the letter *peh*. Why? Because at the center of healing is our mouth.

The Bible tells us that life and death are in the power of the tongue (Proverbs 18:21). The power of praise, the power of declaration, and healing begin with the mouth. Exodus 15:26 tells us, "He [the LORD] said, 'If you listen carefully to the voice of the LORD your God and do what is right in his eyes, if you pay attention to his commands and keep all his decrees, I will not bring on you any of the diseases I brought on the Egyptians, for I am the LORD, who heals you'"

(NIV). This is a season when God wants to bring not just breakthrough; He also wants to bring healing, wholeness, and redemption in our lives. God doesn't want to merely heal our past, our pains, and our problems; He wants to *redeem* them.

> Our stories can make us angry, causing us to disconnect from God, ourselves, and others. Or we can choose to find God in the midst of our pain and suffering.

What does it mean that God wants to heal and redeem our problems? Let me share a story to illustrate the point. I went to speak to a group of kids. As I was speaking, I noticed this one kid, and God told me I needed to talk to him. At one point after my talk, I looked around, and the place was packed. The only empty seat in the entire venue was next to this kid (notice how God works). I sat down next to him, and he told me that what I said impacted him. Then he said, "I've got a problem. I don't believe I can have faith in God anymore, because every person I've ever loved has died. My mom died. My aunt, who is a second mom to me, is sick, and she's dying. Not too long ago, I left being in a gang. I was walking home from school trying to put that gang life behind me, and a former gang member jumped out to shoot me. My best friend pushed me away, and he took the bullet for me, and he died. How can I believe God loves me and wants the best for me and has a plan for my life and all that has ever happened? I'm struggling to believe what you have to say even though I want to believe it."

At first, I wanted to give him some theological answers from the book of Genesis about creation and free will. Thankfully, I realized that wasn't the way to go. So I said to him, "That wasn't God who did those things. God is good, but there are also forces of darkness in this world that come to rob and kill and destroy. God did not take those people from your life. What you need to understand is what you need to do to make things right. You need to get revenge."

He thought I was telling him to take a 9mm and go do some drive-by shooting or something crazy. I told him that wasn't what I was talking about. I said, "Listen, your friend gave his life for you. The Enemy wanted to take your life. The Enemy has taken other people's lives who were close to you. You can get revenge by impacting the lives of the people around you and preventing what has happened to you from happening to them. Every life that you touch, every life that you impact, and every life saved because of your actions is the way God uses you. In one sense, you are stealing them back, getting revenge. You are making a difference. And God is not only redeeming you. He will heal your pain. He will redeem your pain as your story touches the lives of many."

Some of us have stories that include deep hurts, deep pains, and deep losses. Our stories can make us angry, causing us to disconnect from God, ourselves, and others.

Or we can choose to find God in the midst of our pain and suffering. God says in Isaiah 53:11, "After he has suffered, he [Jesus] will see the light of life and be satisfied" (NIV). Why will Jesus be satisfied? Because He knew His death would redeem many. God wants to heal *and* redeem you from your pain and suffering. Your pain wasn't purposeless. There is something good God can bring out of it.

Knowing there's a purpose for pain is part of our healing. God spoke to me one day, and He said, "Holy, holy, holy." Not *wholly*, or *holey* like some pairs of socks. God was saying that we all have holes in our souls. The Hebrew word for *sickness* comes from a root word that means "to bore out or create a hole." Sickness comes when there are holes in our souls like a piece of Swiss cheese. God wants to come in and fill the holes in ways that make us holy and ultimately whole. He takes us from having holes to filling in those holes to making us holy and set apart for His plans and purposes.

We can decide to not dwell on our wounds. We can receive healing and move on to use our story to help others. God wants to exchange brokenness for wholeness. God gives us a way to break through our pain and suffering. He heals us so we can, like that young man I sat with, impact other people's lives and reflect Him to them.

Entrepreneur and lyricist Tim Jahnigen joined British musician Sting to create indestructible soccer balls. According to Sting, they are sending these new soccer balls to "impoverished areas, refugee camps, conflict zones, and

U.N. hotspots all over the world."[14] The problem they solved came from kids playing with regular soccer balls, and the balls would pop and deflate, and the kids could not afford to keep replenishing the balls. The kids were also playing with tin cans and wadded paper. So these two men created a ball that could be stuck with a knife, last thirty years, and never deflate. They have produced well over 50,000 balls and placed them in 120 countries.

Developing and giving away indestructible soccer balls is one example of healing rooted in wholeness. Some people will try to stick you with a knife and poke holes in you. They are going to try to destroy your dreams and deflate you. They are going to try to make you like Swiss cheese. But there is a healing and a wholeness in the Lord that you become so holy, you re-inflate.

The Lord spoke through the prophet Jeremiah and said, "Indeed, I will bring it [the future restored Jerusalem] health and healing, and I will surely heal them. I will reveal to them an abundance of *shalom* and truth. I will restore Judah from exile and Israel from exile, and will rebuild them, as in former times" (Jeremiah 33:6–7). Commenting on this verse, Warren Wiersbe wrote, "The defiled nation would be healed and cleansed (vv. 6–8), and the disgraceful city would bring joy and renown to the Lord and be a testimony to all the

---

14 "Sting Helps Create Indestructible Soccer Ball," *ThePostGame*, November 15, 2012, http://www.thepostgame.com/blog/good-sports/201211/rocker-helps-create-indestructible-soccer-ball.

nations of the world of the marvelous goodness and grace of God."[15] Like the restored city of Jerusalem, we too can be healed and made whole. We can re-inflate and declare how the Lord brought healing, restoration, and wholeness to us.

God has made me whole. Healing and breakthrough are in my DNA. Judah had a son (Genesis 46:12). His name was Peres, and from him ultimately descended Yeshua-Jesus. *Peres* means breakthrough. Yeshua-Jesus is directly related to the son of Judah, whose name means breakthrough. And, ultimately, He is the One who brings breakthrough.

Micah 2:13 says, "One breaking through will go up before them. They will break through, pass through the gate and go out by it. Their King will pass through before them."

What better leader is there than the One who is called here "the Breaker." Just as the Lord went before His people in the pillar of fire and the cloud through the wilderness, so three times in verse 13 we are told He will go before His people to guide them. This Breaker can be none other than the Messiah Himself. It is He who will clear the way for the people to break out of their enemies' cities, passing through as if there were no gates.[16]

---

15 Warren W. Wiersbe, *Be Decisive*, "Be" Commentary Series (Wheaton, IL: Victor Books, 1996), 138.

16 Walter C. Kaiser and Lloyd J. Ogilvie, Micah, *Nahum, Habakkuk, Zephaniah, Haggai, Zechariah, Malachi*, vol. 23, The Preacher's Commentary Series (Nashville, TN: Thomas Nelson Inc, 1992), 46.

The Lord is their head, and the Lord is the one who breaks through. He will clear the way to a breakthrough. Yeshua-Jesus will clear away any hurt and negative natural tendencies. He has broken through for you. You are in Him; His spiritual DNA is in you. That means DNA in you can break through. It's in your genes.

BREAKTHROUGH THINKING IN REVIEW

The decade of 5780 is the decade of the peh and breakthrough; it is the decade of supernatural strength that leads to healing, redemption, and breakthrough. If we let Him, God will break through for us. Every day we can declare our escape from Egypt—what is keeping us in bondage and confinement. Every day we can declare our breakthrough.

Rosh Hashanah is the new year. Most people make resolutions at the new year because how you start your year sets the trajectory for the next twelve months. Right now, you can set the right path. The foundation is holy. God asked not for the best fruits; He asked for the *first* fruits. The first fruits are holy because they set the foundation. They require faith because you don't know what's coming your way in the new year. You only know what you have right now. This decade is a season of bringing the first fruits and setting the best foundation.

This is a season in which we have to understand one more area of breakthrough. This is what Proverbs 3:9–10 says, "Honor ADONAI with your wealth and with the first of your entire harvest. Then your barns will be filled with plenty, your vats will overflow with new wine." The word translated *over-flow* in Hebrew is the word we've been featuring in this book: peres, or breakthrough. This decade is the season of living the breakthrough. On a spiritual level, living out of the overflow means trusting God in all things and expecting Him to give us the breakthrough He's designed for us. Materially, overflow means honoring God with the first fruits of what He has given us.

> Divine breakthrough leads to God's promise to bless us. I've experienced blessing after blessing as I trusted God in faith.

So I pray that by faith we will all sow for the genuine breakthrough of this season to trust and believe God for His very best in our life. I see my breakthroughs, and I pray you see yours as well, with the expectant hope that God is going to do something awesome in your life. Remember, too, that when God gives you the breakthrough, it's never *just* for you. The Messiah broke through for you. Moses had to have the breakthrough within so he could have a breakthrough for his people without. When God gives you the breakthrough, it's to help others break through and see their victory.

Where does our breakthrough lead us?

In the next section we'll take a look at the next step after breakthrough—living in the overflow. God didn't merely deliver the Hebrews out of bondage to exist and wander in a dry, barren desert. God freed them from bondage to give them the Promised Land. God called Abram (later named Abraham) out of Ur and promised him land that would restore the blessings of Eden.

Divine breakthrough leads to God's promise to bless us. I've experienced blessing after blessing as I trusted God in faith. His blessing comes in many forms, and sometimes His blessing isn't what I think it should be, but God always blesses when I obey and follow Him in faith. And His blessing is always for my good.

As we experience breakthrough, we also have the opportunity to experience life in the overflow. As we experience breakthrough, we grow in life, and we also open the door to a transformed life—a life filled with blessing, hope, and faith.

PART 2: LIVING IN THE OVERFLOW

AN INTRODUCTION

I N EVERY SEASON, God wants us to have an extraordinary life. Rather than live by what others might call normal, He calls us to live in the overflow. God wants us to live in abundance, not out of lack. He has called us to impact the world, but if we're living on empty, what is left in us to give and serve others? How can we minister to the world if we're struggling to keep our "gas tanks" full?

We want to help you move from feeling empty to living a life in the overflow. We want you to experience the transformation God has for you. We want you to experience breakthroughs and also live to the full.

We can find one of the most beautiful pictures of the overflow and transformation God wants to build into our lives in John 2:1–11. Often called the Miracle of the Wine or the Miracle at Cana, this was the first of thirty-five major miracles Jesus performed during His earthly ministry.

Why did He attend a wedding? The Bible tells us Jesus and His disciples "were also invited." One writer believes it was because the people in this small village enjoyed being with Jesus. The Holy One wasn't so proud or vain that He could not attend a wedding.

But I also think God had a deeper purpose in mind. His goal was to transform lives. And this little wedding allowed Him to not only kick off His ministry with an amazing miracle, but it also teaches us how to live as His disciples in ways that profoundly influence the world.

In this section of the book, we'll dig deeply into this incredible miracle and learn about living in the overflow. We'll see the breakthrough thinking that occurred that day, and we'll learn how one small moment in the first century can help us live a transformed life.

Are you ready to live a life that overflows? Follow me on this journey and see how it's possible for you and for me to live a life we may never have expected.

8

Water to Wine

On the third day, there was a wedding at Cana in the Galilee. Yeshua's mother was there, and Yeshua and His disciples were also invited to the wedding. When the wine ran out, Yeshua's mother said to Him, "They don't have any wine!"

Yeshua said to her, "Woman, what does this have to do with you and Me? My hour hasn't come yet."

His mother said to the servants, "Do whatever He tells you."

Now there were six stone jars, used for the Jewish ritual of purification, each holding two to three measures. Yeshua said to them, "Fill the jars with water!" So they filled them up to the top. Then He said to them, "Take some water out, and give it to the headwaiter." And they brought it.

Now the headwaiter did not know where it had come from, but the servants who had drawn the water knew. As the headwaiter tasted the water that had become wine, he calls the bridegroom and says to him, "Everyone brings out the good wine first, and whenever they are drunk, then the worse. But you've reserved the good wine until now!" Yeshua did this, the first of the signs, in Cana of the Galilee—He revealed His glory, and His disciples believed in Him. (John 2:1–11)

John's Gospel provides us with an accurate biblical account that is also somewhat different from the other three Gospels. He was an eyewitness who presents personal and precise details. His Gospel's uniqueness shines a sharp and brilliant bright light on Jesus. That was John's purpose. He wanted people to know who Jesus is, and he wanted them to decide between the light of Jesus and the darkness of religion, the world, and their ulterior motivations.

THE THIRD DAY

God didn't waste any words through the pen of John. I believe every word has a particular significance, and therefore, when we see a word, we need to ask why it's there. For example, why was the first miracle performed on the third day of the week?

In Jewish thought, the third day is the day of double blessing. Why? In Genesis 1:10–12, God says it is "good" twice on the third day. Many Jewish weddings in Israel occur on the third day of the week because of this.

The third day is not only a day of double blessing; it's also a day of revelation. Exodus 19:1, 16–17 says, "In the third month after *Bnei-Yisrael* had gone out of the land of Egypt, that same day they arrived at the wilderness of Sinai. . . . In the morning of the *third day*, there was thundering and lightning, a thick cloud on the mountain, and the blast of an exceedingly loud *shofar*. All the people in the camp trembled. Then Moses brought the people out of the camp to meet God, and they stood at the lowest part of the mountain." It was the *third month* from the first Passover in Egypt. Just as God, in Genesis, revealed His glory on the *third day*.

As we continue to read in Exodus, we find that as the Lord spoke to Moses, he went up and down the mountain two or three times in order to relay God's message to the children of Israel. Then the Lord gave Moses specific instructions to prepare the people. Exodus 19:10–11 tells us, "ADONAI said to Moses, 'Go to the people, and sanctify them today and tomorrow. Let them wash their clothing. Be ready for the third day. For on the third day ADONAI will come down upon Mount Sinai in the sight of all the people.'" God reveals the greater glory on the third day for the Hebrews.

In Genesis 40:20–22, we find Joseph interpreting dreams of the cupbearer and baker of Pharaoh. Joseph made it clear that these two dreams would be revealed three days later. God revealed a message through Joseph to these palace officials and revealed it three days later.

> The third day is a day of double blessing. It's a day of revelation and it's a day of salvation, but it's also a day of redemption and resurrection because Jesus rose from the dead on the third day.

One of the most significant and revelatory "third-day events" occurred when God commanded Abraham to take his beloved son Isaac and offer him up as a burnt offering on top of one of the mountains, as God commanded (Genesis 22:1–2). In verse 4 we read, "On the third day, Abraham lifted up his eyes and saw the place from a distance." What day did Abraham lift his eyes and see the mountain? The third day. The third day was a day of revelation and salvation for Abraham and Isaac.

The third day is a day of salvation and breakthrough for the Jewish people. In the book of Esther, when Mordecai (Esther's foster father, as she was his uncle's daughter [Esther 2:7]) discovered Haman's plot to annihilate the Jews by manipulating Ahasuerus the king, he asked Esther to go before the king, but she knew that was unlawful. She told Mordecai, "Go! Gather together all the Jews who are in Shushan and fast for me. Do not eat or drink for three days, night or day.

My maids and I will fast in the same way. Afterwards, I will go in to the king, even though it is not according to the law. So if I perish, I perish!" (Esther 4:16).

It was on the third day that Esther went before the king. She risked her life because of what God revealed to her during the three days. The third day was a significant turning point also for the salvation of the Jews during this time.

The third day is a day of double blessing. It's a day of revelation and it's a day of salvation, but it's also a day of redemption and resurrection because Jesus rose from the dead on the third day. He perfectly fulfills Hosea 6:1–3: "Come, let us return to ADONAI. For He has torn, but He will heal us. He has smitten, but He will bind us up. After two days He will revive us. On the third day He will raise us up, and we will live in His presence. So let us know, let us strive to know ADONAI. Like dawn His going forth is certain. He will come to us like the rain, like the latter rain watering the earth."

Jesus revived and restored on the third day. We will ultimately be raised with Him and experience the power of resurrection. The good news is we can experience that power today, through faith in Him. The Apostle Paul reminds us of this in Romans 6:4: "Therefore we were buried together with Him through immersion into death—in order that just as Messiah was raised from the dead by the glory of the Father, so we too might walk in newness of life." The Apostle Peter expressed a similar thought when he wrote, "Blessed be the God and Father of our Lord *Yeshua* the Messiah! In His great mercy He caused us to be born again to a living hope through the resurrection of Messiah *Yeshua* from the dead" (1 Peter 1:3).

These two verses express a significant truth that believers can embrace and apply if they want to experience breakthrough and overflow. Jesus' resurrection on the third day brings us power, and we can walk in a new life with an expectant and hopeful future in Him.

There is a reason Jesus performed His first miracle on the third day. This supernatural manifestation on the third day prefigured the death and resurrection of the Messiah, revealing His ultimate glory. The third day unlocks the door of belief. The third day brought blessing, revelation, restoration, and resurrection to the disciples, to the people at the wedding, and to us today.

> This supernatural manifestation on the third day prefigured the death and resurrection of the Messiah, revealing His ultimate glory. The third day unlocks the door of belief. The third day brought blessing, revelation, restoration, and resurrection to the disciples, to the people at the wedding, and to us today.

9

Transformation

JESUS' RESURRECTION BRINGS salvation to us (Romans 10:9–10). It is through Jesus that we experience salvation—freedom from sin, condemnation, and a new life. In another of his biblical writings the Apostle John wrote, "And the testimony is this—that God gave us eternal life, and this life is in His Son. The one who has the Son has life; the one who does not have *Ben-Elohim* does not have life." This passage tells us that God has given us eternal life and this life is in His Son, the Messiah, Jesus. In other words, the way to possess eternal life is to possess God's Son.

The challenge for us is that we can experience salvation, but not experience the profound transformation in our lives that God wants for us. Why? Because salvation is the beginning of a process, not the end of the process. God wants us to be with Him eternally, but He also desires us to be transformed. And we can experience that now, in this world. God wants us to experience the overflowing abundance of a transformed life, and to do that, we need His Son, Yeshua-Jesus.

Years ago, there was a very wealthy man who, with his devoted young son, shared a passion for art collecting. Together they traveled around the world, adding only the finest art treasures to their collection. Priceless works by Picasso, Van Gogh, Monet, and many others adorned the walls of the family estate. The widowed elder man looked on with satisfaction as his only child became an experienced art collector. The son's trained eye and sharp business mind caused his father to beam with pride as they dealt with art collectors around the world.

> Because salvation is the beginning of a process, not the end of the process. God wants us to be with Him eternally, but He also desires us to be transformed. And we can experience that now, in this world. God wants us to experience the overflowing abundance of a transformed life, and to do that, we need His Son, Yeshua-Jesus.

As winter approached, war engulfed the nation, and the young man left to serve his country. After only a few short weeks, his father received a telegram. His son was missing in action. The art collector anxiously awaited more news, fearing he would never see his son again. Within days, his fears were confirmed. The young man had died while rushing a fellow soldier to a medic.

Distraught and lonely, the old man faced the upcoming Christmas holidays with anguish and sadness. The joy of the season—a season that he and his son had so looked forward to—would visit his house no longer.

On Christmas morning, a knock on the door awakened the depressed old man. As he walked to the door, the masterpieces of art on the walls only reminded him that his son was not coming home. When he opened the door, he was greeted by a soldier with a large package in his hand. He introduced himself to the man by saying, "I was a friend of your son. I was the one he was rescuing when he died. May I come in for a few moments? I have something to show you."

As the two began to talk, the soldier spoke of how the man's son had told everyone of his, not to mention his father's, love of fine art. "I'm an artist," said the soldier, "and I want to give you this." As the old man unwrapped the package, the paper gave way to reveal a portrait of the son.

Though the world would never consider it the work of a genius, the painting featured the young man's face in striking detail. Overcome with emotion, the old man thanked the soldier, promising to hang the picture over the fireplace. A few hours later, after the soldier had departed, the old man set about his task.

True to his word, the painting went above the fireplace, pushing aside thousands of dollars of paintings. And then the man sat in his chair and spent Christmas gazing at the gift he had been given. During the days and weeks that followed, the man realized that even though his son was no longer with him, the boy's life would live on because of those he had touched. He would soon learn that his son had rescued dozens of wounded soldiers before a bullet stilled his caring heart.

As the stories of his son's gallantry continued to reach him, fatherly pride and satisfaction began to ease the grief. The painting of his son soon became his most prized possession, far eclipsing any interest in the pieces for which museums around the world clamored. He told his neighbors it was the greatest gift he had ever received.

The following spring, the old man became ill and passed away.

The art world was in anticipation. Unmindful of the story of the man's only son, but in his honor, those paintings would be sold at an auction. According to the will of the old man, all of the art works would be auctioned on Christmas Day, the day he had received his greatest gift.

The day soon arrived, and art collectors from around the world gathered to bid on some of the world's most spectacular paintings. Dreams would be fulfilled this day; greatness would be achieved as many claimed, "I have the greatest collection." The auction began with a painting that was not on any museum's list. It was the painting of the man's son. The auctioneer asked for an opening bid. The room was silent.

"Who will open the bidding with one hundred dollars?" he asked.

Minutes passed. No one spoke.

From the back of the room came, "Who cares about that painting? It's just a picture of his son. Let's forget it and go on to the good stuff." More voices echoed in agreement.

"No, we have to sell this one first," replied the auctioneer. "Now, who will take the son?"

Finally, a friend of the old man spoke. "Will you take ten dollars for the painting? That's all I have. I knew the boy, so I'd like to have it."

"I have ten dollars. Will anyone go higher?" called the auctioneer. After more silence, the auctioneer said, "Going once, going twice. Gone."

The gavel fell, cheers filled the room, and someone exclaimed, "Now we can get on with it and we can bid on these treasures!"

The auctioneer looked at the audience and announced the auction was over. Stunned disbelief quieted the room. Someone spoke up and asked, "What do you mean it's over? We didn't come here for a picture of some old guy's son. What about all of these paintings? There are millions of dollars of art here! I demand that you explain what's going on here!"

The auctioneer replied, "It's very simple. According to the will of the father, whoever takes the son . . . gets it all."[17]

---

17 "Whoever Takes the Son Gets It All," *Tony Cook Ministries*, https://www.tonycooke.org/stories-and-illustrations/son _getsitall/.

Nineteenth-century commentator E. W. Rice wrote, "Jesus has given life in overflowing abundance, that they might perceive their enlarged privileges; he opens wide the door of access to God; takes away the vail; allows the soul to come to God through Christ alone; requiring no other priest, sacrifice, or intercessor."[18] Whoever has the Son has it all.

> Looking at people, circumstances, and challenges through the good eye means we embrace Romans 8:28 and believe that when we love and obey Him, He will work all things out for our good.

The Bible shows us two types of life: *bios*, the physical world, and *zōē*, the spiritual world. Jesus tells us in John 10:10, "The thief comes only to steal, slaughter, and destroy. I have come that they might have life, and have it abundantly!" Jesus came to give us *zōē* life—an abundant, overflowing life that is ours if we're willing to seek out this life God has for us.

Enjoying life begins with a choice. Remember, in an earlier chapter, we talked about the ayin—the good eye and the bad eye? Part of seeking out the life God has for us is choosing to look through our good eye. Looking at people, circumstances, and challenges through the good eye means

---

18 Edwin W. Rice, *People's Commentary on the Gospel of John* (Philadelphia, PA: The American Sunday School Union, 1893), 178.

we embrace Romans 8:28 and believe that when we love and obey Him, He will work all things out for our good.

Choosing to look through the good eye gives us freedom. How? Because looking through the good eye frees us from the bondage of trying to live our lives under self-guided plans instead of yielding to the plan He has for us, which is always the best. Remember, the Enemy always seeks to make our lives miserable (1 Peter 5:8). We defeat his plans when we choose the *good eye* and discover God's plan and God's breakthrough for us.

We need to enjoy everyday life, and we need to do life in abundance with God.

10

Keys for Living a Life That Overflows

W<small>E ENDED THE</small> previous chapter talking about how we can live in abundance. In this chapter I want to give three essential keys to living not only an abundant life, but a life that overflows.

FAITH AND TRUST

Faith (*emûnāh* in Hebrew) and trust (*bitachon* in Hebrew) are two essential keys to living in the overflow. God wants us to live in faith and trust so that we may begin to experience this overflow. In John 2, the wine ran out, but Mary had faith and trust in Jesus. She came directly to Him in faith, expecting that He was going to help.

It's interesting to me that the miracle didn't happen until the wine ran out. Many times, when we experience a similar situation, we respond with worry and anxiety. We run around, wringing our hands, wondering what we need to do to solve whatever challenge we're facing. When we begin to live in the overflow, we move from fear, worry, and anxiety, to faith. Then, as we believe, we move from faith to trust that God will show up.

> If we want to live a life in the overflow, we, like Mary at the wedding in Cana, should trust in God and rely on the fact that He will show up in every circumstance.

David wrote Psalm 56 while facing a fearful situation. In fear of his life and seeking refuge from Saul, David hid among the Philistines (1 Samuel 21:10) in Gath (the land of his former enemy, Goliath). When the Philistines recognized him, he feared for his life and escaped by pretending to be insane (1 Samuel 21:11–15).

The future king of Israel was struggling with fear (verse 4). Here we see the mighty warrior and the slayer of Goliath living in terror with no rest and nowhere to go—except to God.

In this beautiful psalm (or prayer), David didn't run from his fear. He didn't wring his hands in worry and fret. David chose to trust God and have faith that He would deliver him. He wrote, "In a day when I am afraid, I will put my trust in You" (Psalm 56:4).

Bible commentator James M. Boice wrote, "He trusts God, whom he calls *Elohim* four times (two times in verse

4, once each in verses 10–11) and Jehovah once (in verse 10). Not man! Not circumstances! Not his own cunning, as useful as that seemed to have been at Gath! He trusts God: 'In God I trust.' It is because of this that he could ask, 'What can man do to me?' and expect the answer, 'Nothing.'"[19]

Candidly, most of us won't face the types of fears David experienced. But we may face the fears of unemployment, health, relationships, and others that to us, in the twenty-first century, probably feel just as fearful. In Psalm 56, we find David living courageously in spite of his fears. He took his concerns to God while in the presence of his enemies—in the middle of his challenges. And if we want to live a life in the overflow, we, like Mary at the wedding in Cana, should trust in God and rely on the fact that He will show up in every circumstance.

The writer of Hebrews reminds us, "Now faith is the substance of things hoped for, the evidence of realities not seen" (Hebrews 11:1). Faith is knowing, deep in your heart, what is coming your way even though it's not yet seen. Faith says, "Whether I can see it today, or understand it in my mind, I *know* what God has promised and I know He *will* do it."

---

19 James Montgomery Boice, *Psalms 42–106: An Expositional Commentary* (Grand Rapids, MI: Baker Books, 2005), 471.

Helen Keller said, "The only thing worse than being blind is having sight but no vision."[20] When we live in the overflow, we can see things on a spiritual level. Like King David and Mary, we have a godly vision based on faith and trust that guides and sustains us. Pastor Jim Cymbala wrote, "Faith alone is the trigger that releases divine power. As Peter wrote, it is 'through faith [that we] are shielded by God's power' (1 Peter 1:5). Our trying, struggling, or promising won't work; faith is what God is after. Faith is key to our relationship with Him."[21] Congregational minister Horace Bushnell commented, "If you go to Christ to be guided, He will guide you; but He will not comfort your distrust or half-trust of Him by showing you the chart of all His purposes concerning you. He will show you only into a way where, if you go cheerfully and trustfully forward, He will show you on still farther."[22]

The foundation of living in abundance and overflow begins and ends with faith and trust.

Twelve Spies

We mentioned these men in an earlier chapter, but their story is worth examining again. Chapters 13 and 14 of the book of Numbers give us a vivid example of spiritual vision.

---

20 Marxus A. Roberts, *Thoughts for Your Day: Meditations food for Contemplation* (Bloomington, IN: AuthorHouse, 2019), eBook edition.

21 Jim Cymbala, *Fresh Faith* (Grand Rapids, MI: Zondervan, 2011), eBook edition.

22 Charles F. Stanley, *Enter His Gates: A Daily Devotional* (Nashville: Thomas Nelson Publishers, 1998).

Let me give you some background before we dig into the story.

The last decade (5770) in the Hebrew calendar was the decade of the ayin, which means "eye." Since Hebrew letters and words have numerical significance, ayin's numerical value is seventy. The significance of the eye involves learning to see differently. Until you learn to see differently, you'll never live a life of breakthrough and overflow. The ayin, like us, has two eyes, and symbolically one is known as the good eye and one is known as the bad eye. We talked about this concept in an earlier chapter, where we referenced Matthew 6:22–23. Yeshua-Jesus talks about the good eye and the bad eye. To refresh our memories, what is the bad eye? It is a pessimistic, negative-thinking eye. The bad eye is always the eye that focuses on the cloud instead of the silver lining. Many Israelites died in Egypt because they were focused (using their bad eye) on staying instead of leaving for the Promised Land with Moses.

Once again, we see the good eye is key to breakthrough and living in the overflow. The good eye sees the blessed life—the good in all people, circumstances, and situations. The good eye directly connects to the brain. Our brains process the information our eyes show it. The connection between our eyes and our brains gives us insight. How we determine to see the world determines how we will process our experiences in this world. That's why two people can look at the same image or situation and come to very different conclusions and understandings.

In the biblical account, twelve spies were sent into Canaan, the Promised Land, to scout out the land. Ten could only see the problems, pitfalls, and everything that was wrong. Only two could see the good. Of the twelve spies who came back, ten gave an unfavorable report. Those ten allowed their bad eye to prevail. They said, "The land is good. It flows with milk and honey. It's amazing. Look at the giant fruit we carried back! It was terrific, *but* . . ."

Friends, *buts* will always get us into trouble. Why do we want to insert *buts* into our thinking and living? God doesn't like *buts*. Our *buts* will rob us of living in the overflow.

The ten spies were afraid of the giants and fortified cities. Their bad eye led to bad thinking. Their bad thinking moved to their mouths (giving a bad report), undermining the children of Israel's faith and causing them to wander in the desert for forty years and die. They bad-mouthed God, His promises, and the land that He promised to give them.

Joshua and Caleb, the two spies who gave the positive report, had a different spirit. They saw from the place of the good eye. They said, "There are giants in the land—so what? There are fortified cities—so what?" They implored the people to listen to God's promises. They had the faith and trust to know God could handle giants and fortified cities. They knew God would empower them to a life of overflow and breakthrough.

However, the Hebrews followed their bad eye instead of their good eye. Joshua and Caleb had faith. They believed. And their belief led them to trust. They were the only two of that generation to enter the Promised Land.

Years later, Caleb, at eighty-five years old, told Joshua, "I want Hebron. I want to go up and take Hebron" (see Joshua 14:12). Remember, Hebron was the place of the giants. At eighty-five years old, Caleb asked for the toughest assignment. Caleb lived a life of overflow. Giants didn't bother him because he had complete faith and trust in God. Warren Wiersbe wrote:

> *Caleb was eighty-five years old, but he didn't look for an easy task, suited to an "old man." He asked Joshua for mountains to climb and giants to conquer! His strength was in the Lord, and he knew that God would never fail him. The secret of Caleb's life is found in a phrase that's repeated six times in Scripture: "he wholly followed the Lord God of Israel" (Josh. 14:14; also see Num. 14:24; 32:12; Deut. 1:36; Josh. 14:8–9). Caleb was an overcomer [or lived in the overflow] because he had faith in the Lord (1 John 5:4).*[23]

---

23 Warren W. Wiersbe, *Be Strong*, "Be" Commentary Series (Wheaton, IL: Victor Books, 1996), 125.

The mind works like a projector. It takes images and magnifies them. We are either going to magnify our problems and situations as the ten spies did, or we will magnify the Lord and His promises to us, as Joshua and Caleb did. We have to have faith. We have a choice to make—we can choose the faith that leads to trust. All twelve spies had faith in God, but only two trusted what He had promised. Trust is faith in action, and we need to act upon our faith.

Twelve Disciples

Yeshua-Jesus sent His disciples away in a boat. After spending time alone in prayer, the boat was already a long way from the land. He came to them by walking on the water, but the disciples were afraid, thinking He was a ghost. Immediately Yeshua-Jesus spoke to them, assuring them not to be afraid.

> Answering [Yeshua], Peter said to Him, "Master, if it's You, command me to come to You on the water." And He said, "Come!" And Peter got out of the boat and walked on the water to go to Yeshua. But seeing the wind, he became terrified. And beginning to sink, he cried out, saying, "Master, save me!" Immediately Yeshua reached out His hand and grabbed him. And He said to him, "O you of little faith, why did you doubt?" When they got into the boat, the wind ceased. And those in the boat worshiped Him, saying, "You really are Ben-Elohim!" (Matthew 14:28–33)

Twelve disciples were in the boat, but only one had the faith and trust to step out of the boat, believing he could walk on water. At that moment, Peter was living in the overflow. He had faith and trust to do something he knew he could not do on his own, but only through God's power.

> We are either going to magnify our problems and situations as the ten spies did, or we will magnify the Lord and His promises to us, as Joshua and Caleb did. We have to have faith.

John Ortberg wrote, "Let Peter's walk stand as an invitation to everyone who, like him, wants to step out in faith, who wants to experience something more of the power and presence of God. Let water-walking be a picture of doing with God's help what I could never do on my own. . . . God asks an ordinary person to engage in an act of extraordinary trust, that of getting out of the boat."[24]

If we want to live in the overflow and experience breakthroughs in our lives, we must have faith and trust in God to get out of the boat and see Yeshua-Jesus with our good eye.

OBEDIENCE

Obey is not a four-letter word. It's another key for us to live out of the overflow.

---

24 John Ortberg, *If You Want to Walk on Water, You've Got to Get Out of the Boat* (Grand Rapids, MI: Zondervan, 2001), 9.

In John 2, Mary tells the servants, "Whatever He tells you to do, do it." Mary's only instruction calls us to do what Jesus calls us to do. Belief and faith lead to obedience, and obedience leads to blessing. We need to faithfully obey the will and Word of God to experience a life of overflow. Those wedding servants got to experience, firsthand, how Jesus makes life better.

> The result of our trusting obedience is breakthrough into a life lived in the overflow of His grace and blessings.

Scottish author and Church of Scotland minister William Barclay wrote, "In every life comes periods of darkness when we do not see the way. In every life come things which are such that we do not see why they came or any meaning in them. Happy are those who in such a case still trust even when they cannot understand."[25]

Chances are the servants didn't know what to do, but Mary did. Her faith and trust led her to tell them to do what Jesus tells them to do. They obeyed, and the results were remarkable. The same is true with our lives as well. The result of our trusting obedience is breakthrough into a life lived in the overflow of His grace and blessings.

We can also again look to Peter's experience when he first met Yeshua-Jesus. What if Peter had said no? He would have missed some awesome demonstrations of divine power over

25 William Barclay, *The Gospel of John*, vol. 2 (Louisville, KY: Westminster John Knox Press, 1975, 2001), 119.

the next three years of ministry with Yeshua. I'm sure the experience was a tremendous faith builder for Peter, but it took obedience to get there. Yeshua said, "Come," and Peter responded to the small request.

> Unless you obey God in all things, you will never know the breakthroughs you could experience. You'll never know the wonderful blessings and the overflowing life you could experience if only you had obeyed God.

In our own lives, when we respond in obedience, our faith grows, and God transforms us. Simon Peter could have spent the rest of his life wondering what would have happened. Instead, he had the experience of being with Yeshua, seeing all that happened, and then leading the early church. All because of saying yes to Jesus.

God can transform our lives. For many, it can mean a change of career, a new location, or other God-directed paths. Are you willing to do what God says when He says to do it? Are you ready to leave consequences and challenges to Him and step out in faith and obedience? The hymn writer expressed it simply: "Trust and obey, for there's no other way to be happy in Jesus, but to trust and obey."[26]

Unless you obey God in all things, you will never know the breakthroughs you could experience. You'll never know the wonderful blessings and the overflowing life you could experience if only you had obeyed God.

---

26 John H. Sammis, *Trust and Obey*, 1887, Public Domain.

CHUTZPAH

Chutzpah is a Hebrew word that has been adopted into Yiddish. It has been defined as holy boldness or audacity. Chutzpah is an antidote to fear. Despite the circumstance of not having any wine for the wedding party, Mary was not going to take no for an answer.

Part of faith is taking risks. God honors the risk. If we don't take risks for God, we will never know what is possible. Like Peter, we need to jump in the water and go toward what God is calling us to do, always remembering that we are not responsible for the results.

Abigail had chutzpah. We find her story in 1 Samuel 25. David sent ten men with a message to Nabal (Abigail's wealthy husband):

> "Go up to Carmel, and when you reach Nabal, greet him in my name. Thus you will say: 'Long life! And shalom to you, shalom to your house and shalom to all that is yours. Now I hear that you have shearers. When your shepherds were with us, we did them no harm and nothing of theirs was missing all the time they were in Carmel. Ask your young men and they will tell you. Therefore, let the young men find favor in your eyes, for we have come on a festive day. So please, give to your servants and to your son David, whatever you find at hand.'" (vv. 5–8)

Nabal (his name means fool), in response to David's message and request, hurled an insult at the future king. David was asking for food, and Nabal rejected his request. Then he insulted David by asking, "Who is this David?" David felt his only recourse was to kill Nabal and all of his men.

At this moment, Abigail sprang into action. Nabal would never approve of his wife's actions, so she moved in secret (1 Samuel 25:20). She interceded on behalf of her foolish husband and protected him from his stupidity. Instead of blaming her husband, Abigail said, "It's my fault. Account this sin to me." She brought food to David and his men as she bowed before him.

Abigail's gesture and speech so moved David that he thanked God for sending her. She kept him from a needless killing and defused an extremely tense situation. "Abigail could function as the patron saint of those who meet difficult situations with clear thinking, decisive action, and risk-taking efforts at reconciliation. What she did took both discernment and courage."[27] Abigail was bold. She had chutzpah.

Brett Ratner is one of Hollywood's most successful filmmakers. Throughout elementary school, Ratner made movies instead of doing traditional homework—a talent that helped him skip ahead two grades. In high school, he cut class to

---

27 Kenneth L. Chafin and Lloyd J. Ogilvie, *1, 2 Samuel*, vol. 8, The Preacher's Commentary Series (Nashville, TN: Thomas Nelson, 1989), 183.

hang out on the set of Brian De Palma's *Scarface*, until Ratner became such a "nuisance" that De Palma cast him as an extra in the film.

After graduating high school early, Ratner was determined to attend New York University Film School, but was told that his unimpressive GPA would prevent him from being accepted. Ratner refused to take no for an answer. After barging into the dean's office with his application, NYU accepted him into the program. At only sixteen years old, Ratner became the department's youngest film major in history.

Ratner's big break came after he met hip-hop impresario Russell Simmons, which resulted in an explosive career directing music videos. Ratner has now directed more than one hundred music videos for artists, including Madonna, Mariah Carey, Jessica Simpson, and P. Diddy.

RatPac Entertainment (Ratner and James Packer's film finance production and media company) has co-financed fifty-two theatrically released motion pictures exceeding $9.3 billion in worldwide box office receipts. RatPac's co-financed films have been nominated for fifty-one Academy Awards, twenty Golden Globes, and thirty-nine BAFTAs, and have won twenty-one Academy Awards, seven Golden Globes, and seventeen BAFTAs.[28]

---

28 "Brett Ratner Biography," *IMDb*, https://www.imdb.com/name/nm0711840/bio?ref_=nm_ov_bio_sm.

Ratner made his feature directorial debut at twenty-six years old with the action comedy hit *Money Talks*. He followed with the blockbuster *Rush Hour* and its successful sequels. He also directed *The Family Man*, *Red Dragon*, *After the Sunset*, *X-Men: The Last Stand*, *Tower Heist*, and *Hercules*.[29] Ratner's success began with chutzpah. We can't make anything happen beyond God's grace and divine empowerment. Our responsibility is to step out of the boat and take the risk.

> We can't make anything happen beyond God's grace and divine empowerment. Our responsibility is to step out of the boat and take the risk.

All of us can feel fearful, and one way to overcome the feeling is to step out in faith. One Bible teacher says, "None of us can do what we need to do without God's help. If we look at only what we think we can do, we will all be frightened; but if we look at Jesus and focus on Him, He will give us the courage to go forward even in the presence of fear."[30] In what areas in your life does God want you to take a risk? If we live out of fear, it will rob us of the overflow and the abundant blessing God has for us. Fear will paralyze us. God does not want us to live in that fear. Paul wrote to Timothy, "For God has not given us a spirit of timidity but of power and love and self-discipline."

29 "Brett Ratner Biography," *IMDb*, https://www.imdb.com/name/nm0711840/bio?ref_=nm_ov_bio_sm.

30 Joyce Meyer, *Trusting God Day by Day: 365 Devotions* (New York, FaithWords, 2012), 81.

11

The Overflow Miracle and Jewish Thought

W HEN WE EXAMINE this miracle in John 2, we need to
fully understand not just the miracle, but how this
miracle fulfills the Old Testament. This understanding helps
us knit together both Testaments and allows us to appreciate
the mind-set of the people at the wedding.

FULFILLMENT OF THE TORAH

Why is Yeshua's first miracle turning the water into wine?
John is demonstrating that Jesus is the fulfillment of the
Torah. In Deuteronomy 18:15, Moses tells the people,
"ADONAI your God will raise up for you a prophet like me
from your midst—from your brothers. To him you must listen." Later, in Deuteronomy 34:10, we discover what kind of
prophet: a prophet who God spoke to face-to-face.

Moses did many signs and wonders, and he spoke to God. However, Yeshua-Jesus is greater than Moses. The writer of the book of Hebrews puts it this way:

> *Therefore, holy brothers and sisters, partners in a heavenly calling, take notice of Yeshua—the Emissary and Kohen Gadol we affirm. He was faithful to the One who appointed Him in His house—as was Moses also. For He has been considered worthy of more glory than Moses, even as the builder of the house has more honor than the house. For every house is built by someone, but the builder of all things is God. Now Moses surely was faithful in all God's house as a servant, for a witness of things to be spoken later. But Messiah, as Son, is over God's house—and we are His house, if we hold firm to our boldness and what we are proud to hope. (Hebrews 3:1–6)*

The *Kohen Gadol* refers to the high priest, the person who held the holiest position in Judaism. This role began with Aaron in Exodus and continued until the destruction of the second temple in AD 70. He acted as the spiritual leader for the Jewish people, and was the only one allowed to enter the Holy of Holies on Yom Kippur. Moses was never the high priest, but Yeshua was and is the High Priest. Hebrews 7:20–21 tells us, "And inasmuch as He was not made priest without an oath (for they have become priests without an oath, but He with an oath by Him who said to Him: 'The Lord has sworn and will not relent, "You are a priest forever according to the order of Melchizedek""(NKJV).

Jesus is our High Priest, willing to offer on a cross what the ancient high priests could not—a sacrifice once and for all that was a sufficient sacrifice for the sins of the whole world. Aaron could not do it. Moses could not do it. Only Yeshua-Jesus could be *that* High Priest.

Yeshua-Jesus is greater than Moses, just as grace is greater than the Law. We need to know and obey God's standards, but we need grace along with faith, trust, and obedience if we're going to live a life in the overflow. Jesus is the Son who is faithful over God's house (Hebrews 3:5). Moses was important. He was the great mediator whom God chose to deliver the Law, but God did not give him full responsibility to manage his house. Moses points the way to the Messiah—to Yeshua-Jesus.

John's Gospel is the book of signs. Unlike the other Gospels, he does not record every miracle of Yeshua. John gives us seven, but each one reminds us of the uniqueness of Yeshua-Jesus. Moses performed miracles, delivered his people from physical slavery, and gave his people the Law. Moses was a great and wonderful man. Still, he pointed to one greater and more wonderful than him, to Jesus the Messiah.

What was Moses' first miracle? He turned water to blood (Exodus 7:20). Yeshua-Jesus, at the wedding, begins the redemption process by a similar sign: turning water not into blood but wine. He came so we'd have life more abundantly

(John 10:10). The promise of the Kingdom is abundant life, and the sign of the Kingdom is new wine (Genesis 49:10–12). Wine directly connects to the promise of this new Kingdom. Amos 9:11–13 tells us fountains drip with sweet wine. Just as He did at the wedding, Yeshua-Jesus brings new sweet wine to us as well. Moses's miracle brought death, but Yeshua-Jesus' new wine brings overflowing life.

Another connection to Moses and the Torah is the amount of time it was dark as Yeshua-Jesus spent His last moments on the cross: *three* hours (Matthew 27:45). What was the ninth plague in Exodus? The darkness plague lasted *three* days (Exodus 10:20–22). Jesus' first miracle was like Moses and the first plague, and we can also see a connection between the last two plagues and the cross as well.

And what was the tenth plague? The death of the firstborn (Exodus 11–12). Yeshua-Jesus is God's firstborn Son (Romans 8:29; Colossians 1:15,18). "When the New Testament writers identify Jesus as God's firstborn and only Son, they are endorsing the idea that the firstborn son introduced in the Old Testament reaches its fulfillment in Christ."[31]

Yeshua-Jesus is the Passover Lamb of God who gave His life for us so judgment will "pass over" us, so we might escape slavery and find life just as the Israelites did. Moses led his people out of bondage, but Jesus leads us into an abundant and overflowing life.

---

31 David Limbaugh, *Finding Jesus in the Old Testament* (New York: Simon & Schuster, 2015), eBook edition.

SIX POTS AT THE WEDDING IN CANA

It's important to note that these were no ordinary pots. Large stone pots (*qalal* in Hebrew, meaning a large stone jar for ritual washing[32]) were not subject to the impurity laws (Leviticus 11:32–35). Clay pots, on the other hand, became unclean and needed to be smashed. Stone pots would not become impure and were often used for storing clean water that would later be used for purification. The Mishnah tells us that during the Roman period (the first centuries BC and AD), purification rituals and stone vessels associated with this practice were extremely common in Judea and Galilee, since purification washing was a frequent Jewish religious rite (John 2:6; 3:25; Mark 7:3–4).

Stone pots were much more expensive to make, but they were more economical because unlike clay pots, they could be reused. Since these are stone pots, we can deduce that this household was either a priestly household or a family concerned with purity.

Stone pots were also challenging to make. They were carved from a single piece of stone (typically soft limestone found in the regions of Judea and Galilee). They also required special lathes used by the Romans to manufacture stone columns. Most stone pots were twenty-five to thirty inches high and held approximately eight to ten gallons.

---

32 *Mishnah Parah* 3:3 and *Eduyot* 7:5.

When reading John's Gospel, we need to be alert to its symbolism, which provides deeper meanings we need to explore. These meanings give us a fuller understanding of what God wants us to know, directly impacting our faith and life as believers in the Messiah. The stone pots at the wedding at Cana are a profound example of this. How many pots were there (John 2:6)? Why were there six and not seven (the number of completion)? Why not eight (the number of new beginnings)?

Here's why six is an integral part of this miracle at Cana. Six is the number of creation. God worked for six days, then rested on the seventh. Six is also the number of man. God created the first man and woman, Adam and Eve, on the sixth day of creation. In Jewish thought, man fell on the sixth day; he ate from the tree on the sixth day. According to the rabbis, man lost six things as a result of the Fall:

1. Their radiance (glorified bodies)
2. Their life
3. Their height

> Six is the number of creation. God worked for six days, then rested on the seventh. Six is also the number of man. God created the first man and woman, Adam and Eve, on the sixth day of creation. In Jewish thought, man fell on the sixth day; he ate from the tree on the sixth day.

4. The produce of the earth (before the Fall, produce would ripen and mature quickly)
5. The fruit of the tree (there were no barren trees in the garden)
6. The luminaries (the divine light)

Yeshua-Jesus' first miracle involved six stone pots because He came as both the Second Adam and Savior to begin to restore what was lost in Eden. Since the Fall happened on the sixth day, the Messiah died on the sixth day, which on the Hebrew calendar is Friday. What makes Good Friday so good is that the Messiah came to restore what we lost in Eden. Not only did the Messiah die on the sixth day, but He was also on the cross for six hours and was even pierced in six places.

Yeshua-Jesus died on a cross, symbolizing a tree. Sin came through a tree from which Adam and Eve stole. On Calvary's cross, God put back on the tree what the first man and woman could not. While on the tree, Yeshua-Jesus was pierced six times:

- His head was pierced with a crown of thorns. Why a crown of thorns? What was the curse of creation? It

was that the ground would produce thorns and this-
tles. He was taking the curse on Himself to restore
the blessing.

- His two hands were pierced because it was our hands
  that stole from the tree.
- His side was pierced because the one taken from
  Adam's side (Eve) led him into temptation.
- His two feet were pierced because Genesis 3:15 says
  the seed of the woman would crush the head of
  the serpent, that "he will crush your head, and you
  will crush his *heel*." As His feet were nailed to the
  tree, Satan said, "What are you going to do now"?
  Satan was mocking the promises of God, but God
  was actually using him to fulfill His promise of
  redemption.

In Hebrew, Genesis 1:1 contains seven words
that correspond to the seven days of creation. The
sixth word of Genesis 1:1 begins with the sixth letter, the letter *vav*. Why is this important? Because
in vav is the conjunction *and* the letter that connects "heaven and earth" in Genesis 1:1. When
Adam and Eve sinned they broke the vav, the connection between heaven and earth. When we sin, we break our connection to God Himself.

vav

God sent Yeshua-Jesus to restore what was lost—to bridge the gap and restore this connection between God and us (2 Corinthians 5:18; Colossians 1:19–20). God wants to have a relationship with us. He wants to reconnect so we can know Him, His promises, and His will for us so we can discover our breakthrough and live out of the overflow.

12

How Can We Live in the Overflow?

GOD WANTS TO TRANSFORM US

G OD TRANSFORMS THE ordinary into the extraordinary.
Water is ordinary, but wine is extraordinary. The
Apostle Paul reminds us in 2 Corinthians 5:17, "Therefore
if anyone is in Messiah, he is a new creation. The old things
have passed away; behold, all things have become new."
Yeshua makes us a new creation on the inside. He wants to
transform us so we can live the life He died to give us. Dr.
Charles Stanley wrote:

> *What must happen is a transforming dependence upon*
> *the power of the Holy Spirit. The victorious life is one*
> *that abides and rests in and yields to the Spirit of God.*
>
> *That does not mean that you fail to pray, work, study,*
> *read, or accept responsibility. It does mean that you do*

these things with reliance upon the power of God to liberate you.

How does that happen? By simple faith that God will do it (just as you were saved) and a submissive, obedient heart that looks to and leans on the Spirit of God.[33]

We so often pursue superficial experiences instead of seeking genuine life transformation. We settle for a program instead of focusing on the transformation only the Holy Spirit can bring—faith, trust, and obedience. Just as we learned with the wedding at Cana, if we want to live in the overflow, we must be willing to be transformed by God rather than merely living an ordinary life. We need to take risks and move out into what God is calling us to do. That is how we break through and live in the overflow.

Yeshua-Jesus did not create us to be ordinary, and He does not see us as ordinary or everyday. It can be hard to believe that God created us to be extraordinary and not ordinary. We often fall into the trap of wanting to be a "me too," wanting to be like everyone else, but candidly, imitation leads to limitation. God created each of us to be a unique work of art, and we struggle with that idea. We need the grace to believe what God has said about us, and we need to remember the words of Psalm 139:14: "I praise You, for I am awesomely,

33 Charles F. Stanley, *Enter His Gates: A Daily Devotional* (Nashville: Thomas Nelson Publishers, 1998).

wonderfully made! Wonderful are Your works—and my soul knows that very well." Or, Paul's words from Ephesians 2:10: "For we are God's handiwork, created in Christ Jesus to do good works, which God prepared in advance for us to do" (NIV).

Remember, you are unique. You are God's handiwork. You are not a mistake. There are many things you can do that no one else can. God put you here to be unique and to do unique things. You need a transformed mind that enables you to see what's right about you, and to help you stop looking at what's wrong with you. When you let God transform the way you think about your-self, you can change the way others feel about you. Then your circumstances and challenging situations can change as well.

It can be hard to believe that God created us to be extraordinary and not ordinary. We often fall into the trap of wanting to be a "me too," wanting to be like everyone else, but candidly, imitation leads to limitation. God created each of us to be a unique work of art, and we struggle with that idea.

We need His Spirit to transform our thinking. Pastor Lloyd J. Ogilvie wrote:

> *The Holy Spirit's sealing begins a lifelong process of transformation to our thinking, character, values, and goals. He presses the seal of Christ into our daily*

lives. . . . Our Counselor convicts us of any mani-
festations of pride, self-centeredness, and resistance
to receive love, giving us the courage to change with
His help.[34]

When believers in Yeshua live in the power of the Holy
Spirit, there is supernatural transformation that leads to an
abundant life. When you al-
low the Holy Spirit to transform your thinking, you'll
experience a presence and
power in your life as never before imaginable.

We all need transforma-
tion if we expect breakthrough
and a life that overflows. We
all experience seasons where
we have spiritual battles, bad
attitudes, doubt, and fear.
However, lasting transformation can happen because of what
Jesus promised us (John 16:7) in the person and power of the
Holy Spirit.

> The Bible has survived
> time, criticism, and
> persecution. It deals with
> sin and failures as well
> as heroes. It has had a
> significant influence on
> governments, culture,
> literature, and the arts.
> God's Word is inerrant
> and infallible.

We absolutely must believe and trust God's Word. Paul,
writing to the young pastor Timothy, said, "All Scripture
is inspired by God and useful for teaching, for reproof, for

34 Lloyd John Ogilvie, *Experiencing the Power of the Holy* Spirit
(Eugene, OR: Harvest House Publishers, 2013), 38.

restoration, and for training in righteousness, so that the person belonging to God may be capable, fully equipped for every good deed" (2 Timothy 3:16–17). In this short sentence Paul tells us that God is the source of the Word. The Bible is God-breathed. Only two things have the breath of God. The soul of man and the Word of God. This makes both eternal and highly precious to the Lord.

The study of God's Word breathes new life into our soul and empowers change and transformation. No one can deny the greatness of the Bible. It is the best-selling book of all time. It was written over sixteen hundred years by more than forty authors, in different circumstances and different styles. The Bible covers scores of subjects in three different languages. And when people read it, their lives are changed. It is the living Word of God, and like no other book, a person can read a section at one time in their life and then read the same section years later and hear a fresh message from God.

The Bible has survived time, criticism, and persecution. It deals with sin and failures as well as heroes. It has had a significant influence on governments, culture, literature, and the arts. God's Word is inerrant and infallible.

In studying the written Word of God, we are equipped to faithfully hear the Word of God that is spoken to our hearts. Many blessings can come to us when we are open to hearing God and His transformation for our lives. One morning I was getting ready, and God said to me, "Jason, you are my favorite son."

I said, "Thank you."

God then said, "When you go out there to speak, tell my people that you are my favorite son."

I replied, "I can't do that. The people will pick up stones and stone me."

God said, "Jason, you are a father, and I am a father, but I'm not a father like you are a father. I am the Infinite Father. I can have an infinite number of number one sons and daughters." Knowing this about God is what makes us so exceptional.

Can you believe you are God's number one son or daughter? He can have an infinite number of number one sons and daughters. We are unique.

God loves and values us. He wants to transform us, not only so we reflect Him, but so that we might use the gifts He's given us to serve Him and others. God transforms and employs ordinary people to do extraordinary things—fishermen, tax collectors, and people in our own time like civil rights activist Rosa Parks—men and women living in the overflow.

Rosa Parks was an ordinary woman who was an ordinary seamstress who changed the course of the civil rights movement in the United States. Biography.com tells the story:

> On December 1, 1955, Parks was arrested for refusing a bus driver's instructions to give up her seat to a white passenger. She later recalled that her refusal wasn't

because she was physically tired, but that she was tired of giving in.

After a long day's work at a Montgomery department store, where she worked as a seamstress, Parks boarded the Cleveland Avenue bus for home. She took a seat in the first of several rows designated for "colored" passengers.

The Montgomery City Code required that all public transportation be segregated and that bus drivers had the "powers of a police officer of the city while in actual charge of any bus for the purposes of carrying out the provisions" of the code. While operating a bus, drivers were required to provide separate but equal accommodations for white and black passengers by assigning seats.

This was accomplished with a line roughly in the middle of the bus separating white passengers in the front of the bus and African American passengers in the back. When an African American passenger boarded the bus, they had to get on at the front to pay their fare and then get off and re-board the bus at the back door.

As the bus Parks was riding continued on its route, it began to fill with white passengers. Eventually, the bus was full and the driver noticed that several white passengers were standing in the aisle. The bus driver stopped the bus and moved the sign separating the two sections back one row, asking four black passengers to give up their seats.

The city's bus ordinance didn't specifically give drivers the authority to demand a passenger to give up a seat to anyone, regardless of color. However, Montgomery bus drivers had adopted the custom of moving back the sign separating black and white passengers and, if necessary, asking black passengers to give up their seats to white passengers. If the black passenger protested, the bus driver had the authority to refuse service and could call the police to have them removed.

Three of the other black passengers on the bus complied with the driver, but Parks refused and remained seated. The driver demanded, "Why don't you stand up?" to which Parks replied, "I don't think I should have to stand up." The driver called the police and had her arrested.[35]

Her act of brave defiance began the civil rights movement. Her action transformed laws and effectively began the

---

35 "Rosa Parks Biography," *Biography*, January 17, 2020, https://www.biography.com/activist/rosa-parks.

movement to end legal segregation. Rosa Parks has been an inspiration to many people. That day in Montgomery was just ordinary, and she was an ordinary woman. She probably didn't think that by taking a seat she'd be taking a stand that birthed a national movement.

> God used this ordinary woman to do something extraordinary. She stood up for what was right. When you think of breakthrough and living in the overflow, you will never know how God will use you.

A young pastor named Martin Luther King Jr. heard about her arrest and wound up calling for a boycott of 381 days. The Montgomery bus boycott was a huge success and brought attention to the world. In time, the Supreme Court struck down the Montgomery city code, declaring segregation on public transit systems to be unconstitutional. God used this ordinary woman to do something extraordinary. She stood up for what was right. When you think of breakthrough and living in the overflow, you will never know how God will use you.

GOD WANTS US TO LIVE WITH AN ABUNDANT MIND-SET

We need to develop a John 10:10 mind-set that says, "The thief comes only to steal, slaughter, and destroy. I have come that they might have life, and have it abundantly!" We need to live in the overflow, not in the shortage or out of the lack.

After Yeshua-Jesus turned the water into wine, there was more wine than they needed. The stone pots overflowed, and there was enough wine for the future. When God multiplied the loaves and the fishes (Mark 6:30–44), there was some left over. There's always more than enough with God. No matter how difficult the situation, we have to understand that God is generous, He is good, and He desires to bless us. He wants us to have a prosperity of our souls—spiritually, emotionally, and relationally. He also provides for our needs according to the riches that are in His Son.

If we are going to live in the overflow, we cannot live seeing the pots of our lives as merely empty and focusing on those problems. During a challenging situation, Mary chose to see those empty pots as possibilities! Your challenges contain possibilities for the future. It means stepping out in faith, trusting, and obeying God. It means living with a transformed, abundant-life mind-set.

Yeshua uses the word *abundant* in John 10:10. The Greek word is *perissós*. It means superabundance and overflowing, and far beyond what is necessary. The vision is a pot that is flowing over its brim, or a hole in the ground that is filled up so much that there's a mound on top. Yeshua gives a life that is not constricted but an overflowing life that's over-the-top.

It's possible to have a negative mind-set and a negative attitude that is destroying your life. Bible teacher E. Stanley Jones wrote:

The generation of people that lived on denials soon found themselves disillusioned even with their disillusionments. They had "three sneers for everything and three cheers for nothing." And they soon found they could not live by their sneers; to live by sneers is poor fare. If we should walk to the table each day and look over the food and then turn away in high disdain, we could get away with this disdainful attitude for awhile, but only for awhile. In the end, hunger would bite us and drive us to affirm something about food and to act on our affirmation. Both physically and spiritually, we are positive beings and cannot live by no; we must live by yes. And that yes must be God, or it will let us down.[36]

> Mary chose to see those empty pots as possibilities! Your challenges contain possibilities for the future.

Moses, in Deuteronomy 30:19–20, says, "I call the heavens and the earth to witness about you today, that I have

---

36 E. Stanley Jones, *Abundant Living: 364 Daily Devotions* (Nashville, TN: Abingdon Press, 2014), eBook edition.

set before you life and death, the blessing and the curse. Therefore, choose life so that you and your descendants may

> We can think good or bad thoughts. It's our choice. One leads to a better life; the other leads to a poor life. God gives us free will to choose, and He also gives us the answer— choose life!

live, by loving ADONAI your God, listening to His voice, and clinging to Him. For He is your life and the length of your days, that you may dwell on the land that ADONAI swore to your fathers—to Abraham, to Isaac and to Jacob—to give them." We can think good or bad thoughts. It's our choice. One leads to a better life; the other leads to a poor life. God gives us free will to choose, and He also gives us the answer—choose life!

We can't change some circumstances, but we can improve our outlook. We may not be responsible for the situation we find ourselves in, but only God can fix it. We can knock on God's door and find the help to be transformed and live the abundant life Yeshua calls us to live.

GOD WANTS US TO LEARN TO SEE THE GOOD

Most people at the wedding would have been upset about the sudden shortage of wine. Hospitality in Middle Eastern culture is significant. Running out of wine would have disturbed the guests and made the host feel horrible. Mary knew how to handle the situation, and, instead of worrying about it, she saw the good; she believed *before* seeing.

Most people look at empty pots and think they're out of luck. Mary believed, and that led to her seeing the miracle. Our faith impacts our situations and circumstances. Mary believed and saw; she didn't see and then believe. Faith is about seeing what's not there. We will never be more than we can see if we don't know who God created

> Mary knew how to handle the situation, and, instead of worrying about it, she saw the good; she believed *before* seeing.

us to be, our identity in Him. If we can't see the potential that He has placed in us, if we can't see from the *good eye*, we will never live in the overflow.

We must have the faith to believe, risk, and do things. Psalm 27:14 tells us to see the goodness of God in the land of the living. Do we believe that we will see God's goodness no matter what people, situations, or circumstances tell us? There are days when we don't know how we will pay the bills, and yet He always shows up. He is good all the time. We have to learn to see His good in everything, no matter what circumstances may tell us we are seeing.

Paul wrote in 1 Thessalonians 5:16–18, "Rejoice always, pray constantly, in everything give thanks; for this is God's will for you in Messiah *Yeshua*." Eugene Peterson, in the *Message Bible,* renders "rejoice always" as "Be cheerful no matter what." One commentator wrote, "Joy is that feeling of delight which arises from the possession of present good, or from the anticipation of future happiness; and in both respects the believer has abundant reason for constant joy."[37]

When we fully understand all that Yeshua-Jesus has done for us, when we realize we are forgiven and have the gift of eternal life in Him, when we comprehend His promise that all things will work together for our good—*then* we can live life in the overflow and have the joy that comes from seeing the good in things.

GOD WANTS US TO UNDERSTAND THAT PRESSING LEADS THE BLESSING

We can be in seasons where we feel squeezed, but God wants us to know that out of the squeezing comes the blessing. Pressing produces exceptional wine. In Hebrew, the word *wine* has a numerical value of seventy. The numerical value for the word for *hidden* or *mystery* is also seventy. The numerical value of the word *eyes* is seventy.

> Yayin - wine - 70
> ayin - eye - 70
> sod - hidden mystery - 70

Why is this important for us to understand? The connection is that grapes have an inner potential we can't see.

---

37 H. D. M. Spence and Joseph Exell, Editors, *The Pulpit Commentary* (Peabody, MA: Hendrickson Publishers, 1985), E-sword electronic edition.

It's hidden and a mystery. We see them on the vine. Grapes may look pretty, but it isn't until they are crushed that we discover their hidden potential. Pressing releases what is inside the grape, and our eyes can see the fulfillment of the crushing.

We need to train our eyes to see the mystery that by pressing God brings the blessing. The pressing (life circumstances and situations) exposes our potential and our purpose. Like a grape or an olive, God wants to squeeze out every bit of potential and purpose in our life. We have to go through the crushing to create something more meaningful. If we can survive with a mediocre life, and not do anything meaningful or significant, maybe we don't need the crushing. But if we want the fullness of what Yeshua-Jesus purchased and created us for, we have to experience the pressing.

Jacob gives us an excellent example of this. After stealing the blessing from his brother Esau, fleeing from his home, living with an unscrupulous uncle (who was as tricky and deceitful as Jacob), he made a decision. Years after Jacob had seen his brother, God told him that he must face Esau, whom he assumed would try to kill him. To defend himself, Jacob divided his camp, and he was so nervous that he stayed up all night. An angel came and wrestled with him, ultimately leaving Jacob transformed. At the end of their wrestling match, the angel "struck the socket of [Jacob's] hip" (Genesis 32:26). Jacob's transformation came from being pressed. His later blessings came from the crushing and pressing of God.

Often our most noteworthy victories come out of the ashes of our greatest pressings. As soon as Jacob was crippled, he was able to hang on to the Lord for dear life. He realized that if God didn't bless him, he had no hope. Jacob clung to the Lord. And, sticking to the Lord in brokenness, Jacob received the very blessing he had been scheming to get all his life. Jacob's life was transformed. He was pressed, and out of his pressing came blessing. That is what God did for Jacob, and that's what He will do for you and me.

> God can not only multiply our gifts, talents, and abilities, but He can also supernaturally mature them as well.

GOD GIVES US NEW-OLD WINE

Now the headwaiter did not know where it had come from, but the servants who had drawn the water knew. As the headwaiter tasted the water that had become wine, he calls the bridegroom and says to him, "Everyone brings out the good wine first, and whenever they are drunk, then the worse. But you've reserved the good wine until now!" Yeshua did this, the first of the signs, in Cana of the Galilee—He revealed His glory, and His disciples believed in Him. (John 2:9–11)

The wine Jesus gave them was new, but it tasted old. People who know and enjoy wine know that new wine is *not* good wine. Old wine, appropriately aged, is better. In ancient Middle Eastern celebrations, the host brought out the good wine first. Then, as the party continued, they would serve the more inferior newer wine. Part of the miracle in Cana was that there was a supernatural acceleration in the maturation of the wine. It was new wine, but it tasted like finely aged wine.

Similarly, God can not only multiply our gifts, talents, and abilities, but He can also supernaturally mature them as well. Like sponges, we soak in God's Word and presence because saturation leads to maturation. We need to lean into Him and trust Him to not only show us our gifts but to expand them so we can do far more, with His help, than we thought possible.

A key aspect of this miracle was that Yeshua created new-old wine. The wine was brand new, but it tasted old, like fine aged wine. New-old is even better than old wine. By creating new-old wine, the Messiah was communicating a deeper spiritual truth. The type of wine connects to another lesson Yeshua taught about the old and new.

Yeshua-Jesus was speaking about old and new in Matthew 13:52. He said to them, "Therefore every *Torah* scholar discipled for the Kingdom of heaven is like the master of a household who brings out of his treasure both new things and old." In the Kingdom, there are new treasures and old. Scribes, or Torah scholars, were specifically conversant with the Torah, the five books of Moses. Their focus was understanding the teachings of Moses and how God's commandments apply to every aspect of life. Scribes were expert in the Old, the Hebrew Scriptures. A disciple of Yeshua, on the other hand, should know how to connect the Old with the New. Disciples who are called to be scribes for the Kingdom don't settle for one or the other.

Today, many Jews settle for the Old Testament, and many Christians settle for the New Testament. We find the full inheritance by connecting the old and new—Jew and Gentile coming together and uniting in the Messiah. We shouldn't settle for half an inheritance; we shouldn't settle for old wine. We should accept the new wine and the fullness of what God has.

GOD WANTS US TO KNOW THE BEST IS YET TO COME

"You've reserved the good wine until now!" (John 2:10).

Even during the famine in Egypt, God called Joseph. God had a plan, and He chose one man who loved, trusted, and obeyed Him even when dark circumstances surrounded him. God had something better for Joseph and the Israelites.

God has something better for us too, and we need to have faith and trust that the best is yet to come. We must believe it. God calls us to be people of hope and to rise above our circumstances.

The psalmist tells us in Psalm 71:5–6, "For You are my hope, Adonai my Lord—my trust from my youth. From my birth I have leaned on You. You took me out of my mother's womb. My praise is always about You." Do you wake up every morning saying, "Today is going to be my day!"? If you have a best-is-yet-to-come mindset, you will. God wants us to be expectant on purpose. He wants us to have hope.

> God has something better for us too, and we need to have faith and trust that the best is yet to come. We must believe it. God calls us to be people of hope and to rise above our circumstances.

What is hope? It is the happy anticipation of good. It is an extremely favorable expectation. Hope releases joy, creativity, and an openness to God and His plans for us. We can't live in faith and at the same time talk about what won't happen. We can't just let things happen. Let today be the day you choose to have hope instead of negativity. Let today be the day you live knowing (not just wishing) that the best is yet to come.

It has been reported that on November 18, 1995, Itzhak Perlman, the violinist, came on stage to give a concert at Avery Fisher Hall at Lincoln Center in New York City. If you have ever been to a Perlman concert, you know that getting on stage is no small achievement for him. He was stricken with polio as a child, and so he has braces on both legs and walks with the aid of two crutches.

To see him walk across the stage one step at a time, uncomfortably and slowly, is an unforgettable sight. He walks painfully yet majestically until he reaches his chair. Then he sits down slowly, puts his crutches on the floor, undoes the clasps on his legs, and tucks one foot back and extends the other foot forward. Then he bends down and picks up the violin, puts it under his chin, nods to the conductor, and proceeds to play.

By now, the audience was used to this ritual. They sat quietly while he made his way across the stage to his chair. They remained reverently silent while he undid the clasps on his legs. They waited until he was ready to play.

But this time, something went wrong. Just as he finished the first few bars, one of the strings on his violin broke. You could hear it snap—it went off like gunfire across the room. There was no mistaking what that sound meant. There was no mistaking what he had to do.

People who were there that night thought to themselves, *We figured that he would have to get up, put on the clasps again, pick up the crutches, and limp his way off stage—to either find another violin or else find another string for this one.*

But he didn't. Instead, he waited a moment, closed his eyes, and then signaled the conductor to begin again. The orchestra began, and he played from where he had left off. And he played with such passion and such power and such purity as they had never heard before.

Of course, most people know that it is impossible to play a symphonic work with just three strings. I know that, and you know that, but that night Itzhak Perlman refused to know that. You could see him modulating, changing, and recomposing the piece in his head.

At one point, it sounded like he was de-tuning the strings to get new sounds from them that they had never made before. When he finished, there was an awesome silence in the room. And then people rose and cheered. There was an extraordinary outburst of applause from every corner of the auditorium. Everyone was on their feet, screaming and cheering, doing everything they could to show how much they appreciated what he had done.

He smiled, wiped the sweat from this brow, raised his bow to quiet them, and then he said, not boastfully, but in a quiet, pensive, reverent tone, "You know, sometimes it is the artist's task to find out how much music you can still make with what you have left."[38] We may feel we only have three strings, but God can make music with what remains. We need to give Him our life. Live out of the overflow, take what God has given us, and, by His grace, transcend the loss and make music with what remains.

God didn't create us to be ordinary but extraordinary. He created us to live in the overflow—to live a life of belief that leads to trust that leads to obedience. When we live an overflowing life, God will transform us into a new creation in Christ, ready to seek and serve Him in all things.

---

38 Excerpted from the 1995 *Houston Chronicle* story based on the incident. It is a moving story, but no one has been able to confirm it. The website snopes.com calls it false and cites evidence to support that claim. Nevertheless, the story has been repeated in various places; there was even a book written called *The Broken String*, using the story as its basis. Perlman himself has never confirmed that the event happened.

Epilogue

I N THIS BOOK, we've been talking about breakthroughs and living in the overflow. Right now is the time for you to decide that you want to live life in the full. I have tried to open the door for you to break through all that is keeping you captive. We've journeyed together through Scriptures and stories with one goal in mind—to give you the freedom you need to live your life in overflow.

> Submerge the Bible into your brain. Examine the words and ask Him to show you what they are telling you.

Yeshua-Jesus came to this earth to give you an abundant life. It's time for you to choose life, as we just learned from Moses. Here are some necessary steps to get you started.

STEP ONE: STUDY GOD'S WORD

Your first step in the process is to begin studying God's Word. I don't mean just reading the Bible and checking off your progress. I suggest you need to dig into God's Word and study it carefully. Submerge the Bible into your brain. Examine the words and ask Him to show you what they are telling you.

When you study His Word, it becomes easier to understand His will, His character, and His ways. When you study the Word, you can feel His presence and bring to mind His promises when you are in doubt or conflict with the devil.

There's no doubt in my mind that the Bible will change your life. It changed mine, and it's transformed millions of other people. Psalm 19:8–9 tells us, "The *Torah* of ADONAI is perfect, restoring the soul. The testimony of ADONAI is trustworthy, making the simple wise. The precepts of ADONAI are right, giving joy to the heart. The *mitzvot* of ADONAI are pure, giving light to the eyes."

Contained in this beautiful psalm are nine action statements about the Bible, and they give us nine good reasons why we need to know and study the Scriptures:

1. The Bible restores our soul. The Bible is God's agent to save souls. The more we read the Bible, the more God will reveal Himself to us and restore (or transform) our thinking and our lives.
2. The Bible renews our mind. The Bible is full of practical advice. Its sixty-six books contain God's wisdom for us to do life.
3. The Bible rejoices our heart. The truth is the best way to lift our spirits.
4. The Bible refocuses our vision. Reading and studying the Bible gives us enlightened eyes. We begin to see

more things through our good eye and have clarity on God's direction and plan.

5. The Bible reinforces our life. The Bible doesn't change, and it doesn't fail. It's never out of date. Its precepts are right for us to live holy and overflowing lives.

6. The Bible helps us replace our doubts. God's judgment is true. When we accept Yeshua as Messiah, we have no doubts about our present or our future. We can live in the hope of leaning on God's truth.

7. The Bible will reorder our values. When we spend time studying God's Word, we find that things that were important to us in the past are not essential to us today. We find we have the heart to love and serve people.

8. The Bible will redirect our path. The Bible is full of warnings and promises. We can choose the way of the promises and experience joy and fulfillment. God will set us on a path, and while it may be difficult, it will also be rewarding.

9. The Bible rewards our obedience. Keeping God's Word rewards us. When we do what He wants us to do, all fear will be gone. We can be God's person in the center of His will.

Yeshua-Jesus tells us John 8:31–32, "If you abide in My word, then you are truly My disciples. You will know the truth, and the truth will set you free!" Yeshua is telling us directly how we achieve breakthrough and live in the overflow. We must get the knowledge of God's Word in us. Why? Because when we do, we will be free.

STEP TWO: BE COMMITTED TO PRAYER

The Apostle Paul was an extraordinary figure in the world. One of the many things he did was leave us a legacy through his letters to various churches. While we can glean a better understanding of doctrine or encouragement from his letters, they also give us a rather clear view of how the Apostle prayed. Not only did his prayers chill the heat of Roman Empire paganism and dramatically impact the ancient world, but they also served to encourage and teach the newly formed Christian church to pray and pray fervently.

When we read Paul's letters, we realize he prayed constantly. We read in both 2 Thessalonians 1:11–12 and Romans 1:9–12 of Paul's commitment to pray "without ceasing." This Greek phrase speaks of a tickle in the throat. Pastor Jon Courson wrote, "In other words, to pray without ceasing means to go through the day praying as often and as reflexively as you would cough to suppress a tickle in your throat."[39]

---

39 Jon Courson, *Jon Courson's Application Commentary* (Nashville, TN: Thomas Nelson, 2003), 868.

Paul mentions praying unceasingly so many times in his epistles that we can assume that part of his life's adventure was to pray whenever and wherever. Gregory of Nyssa underscored this thought when he wrote, "Prayer is the delight of the joyful as well as the solace of the afflicted. Prayer is intimacy with God and contemplation of the invisible. . . . Prayer is the enjoyment of things present and the substance of the things to come."[40]

> Paul prayed often and he prayed for people. He experienced horrible circumstances and he experienced blessings, but he never stopped praying.

It's also interesting to note that Paul doesn't pray for things. In his prayers for the church, there is no mention of material provision, safety, fulfilling relationships, or increased converts. To Paul, success in ministry was something that sprang from his deep love of God and God's people, so his prayers reflected that. We read in 1 Thessalonians 3:9, "How can we thank God enough for you in return for all the joy we have in the presence of God because of you?" (NIV). How would people feel if you told them you were praying that for them?

Paul prayed often and he prayed for people. He experienced horrible circumstances and he experienced blessings, but he never stopped praying. He broke through in so many

---

40 William Barclay, *The Letter to the Romans*, 3rd ed., fully revised and updated, *The New Daily Study Bible*, (Louisville, KY: Westminster John Knox Press, 2002), 20.

ways to take the message of Jesus to the Gentiles. In poverty he lived in the overflow of God's grace, protection, and peace. He fought through a "thorn in the flesh," knowing full well God was with him and would give him the strength to endure and press on.

Not only did Paul know God's Word from the Torah to the Prophets, he prayed all the time. And if we expect to break through and live in the overflow, we should as well.

STEP THREE: DECLARE THE PROMISES OF GOD

This is the year and the decade of the peh. God spoke the world into being. There is power in our peh—our mouth. Our mouth must declare both the biblical as well as the personal promises that have been spoken over our lives. By faith we need to call forth things that are not, as if they were. Faith is agreement with God and His promises.

False faith is fear based and is agreement with the lies and the Liar. Yeshua-Jesus in John 8:44 tells us Satan is a liar. He does not stand for the truth. Why? There is no truth in him. Lying is part of his very existence. We need to stop agreeing with the lies that Satan can put into our head and come into alignment with the Word of God and His promises. Then we need to come into agreement with the Lord by using our mouths to declare those promises.

There is also great benefit in asking others to come into agreement with those promises and declare them with us. Don't underestimate or minimize the power of our peh, our mouth, for releasing God's blessing into our life and the lives of others.

> False faith is fear based and is agreement with the lies and the Liar.

By some counts, there are over six thousand promises contained in God's Word. All of these are available to us and can be declared by us. God's promises cover every aspect of our lives. Are you facing an illness? Declare Psalm 103:2-3: "Bless ADONAI, O my soul, forget not all His benefits: He forgives all your iniquity. He heals all your diseases." Do you need comfort or rest? Declare Matthew 11:28-29: "Come to Me, all who are weary and burdened, and I will give you rest. Take my yoke upon you and learn from me, for I am gentle and humble in heart, and 'you will find rest for your souls.'"

[The] power in the promises is about applying God's Word in your unique situations and trials. It's about ceasing to think (and react) like men and women who don't have a trustworthy God and beginning to act like those who have a heavenly Father who watches over every circumstance. It's about leaving the spiritual poverty behind and taking up the treasures of God's Word. It's about developing the practice of looking to the Bible and

extracting promises that were meant for us and then speaking and praying them into our lives.[41]

STEP FOUR: REFUSE TO BE DISCOURAGED BY YOUR FRIENDS

When David was about to fight the giant Goliath, who ridiculed his effort before the battle? His brother Eliab. Sadly, we can't always count on our friends and family to give us the support we need to break through and live in the overflow. Whenever we are doing something great for God, we will hear from people close to us all the reasons why we will fail.

Preparing for this challenge would be your best decision. Don't let defensiveness or jealousy of others stop you from what God is leading you to do. It will take determination on your part, but with God's Word in your mind, and prayer, you'll achieve the breakthrough He has for you. David referenced God's strength nine times before he battled Goliath. His thoughts were not on his brother's criticism or Saul's doubts. God's Word and promises anchored his mind.

When God has called you to breakthrough, have you been negatively influenced by your friends or family? The question is, are they all that you see? Through studying the Bible and prayer, you know His voice, but is that all you hear? Friends' and family's comments can make it harder to hear from the

---

41 Nick Harrison, *Power in the Promises: Praying God's Word to Change Your Life* (Grand Rapids, MI: Zondervan, 2014), eBook edition.

Lord. We need to be like David and major in God. He sees the giant, he hears the criticisms and doubts, but he focuses fully on God. How would majoring in God and the work of the Holy Spirit help you to shrink away from negative criticism and other things that keep you confined?

David ignored the criticism of others, and he faced the giant Goliath. Pastor Max Lucado wrote:

> Don't let defensiveness or jealousy of others stop you from what God is leading you to do. It will take determination on your part, but with God's Word in your mind, and prayer, you'll achieve the breakthrough He has for you.

David's brothers cover their eyes, both in fear and embarrassment. Saul sighs as the young Hebrew races to certain death. Goliath throws back his head in laughter, just enough to shift his helmet and expose a square inch of forehead flesh. David spots the target and seizes the moment. The sound of the swirling sling is the only sound in the valley. Ssshhhww. Ssshhhww. Ssshhhww. The stone torpedoes through the air and into the skull; Goliath's eyes cross and legs buckle. He crumples to the ground and dies. David runs over and yanks Goliath's sword from its sheath, shish-kebabs the Philistine, and cuts off his head.

You might say that David knew how to get a head of his giant.[42]

David broke through. He called upon God for strength. He refused to be distracted or discouraged by his friends. I'm confident you can too.

Study the Word. Be in prayer fervently and unceasingly. Be bold, trust God, live in expectant hope for your breakthrough, and a life that overflows.

Shalom,

Rabbi Jason Sobel

---

42 Max Lucado, *Facing Your Giants: God Still Does the Impossible* (Nashville, TN: Thomas Nelson, 2006), 6.

CREATED FOR *Connection*

A SABBATH SUPPER CLUB GUIDE

by Rabbi Jason Sobel

A Daring Rescue:

THE ORIGINS OF PASSOVER
by Rabbi Jason Sobel

FREE E-BOOK!

TEXT
"TORAH"
to 33777

fusionglobal.org

    @rabbijasonsobel

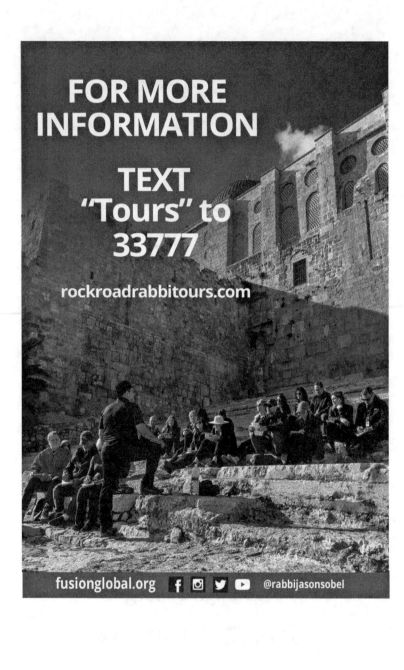

FUSION WITH RABBI JASON
fusionglobal.org

The Fusion website contains ways you can learn more about Rabbi Jason Sobel as well as subscribe to his various teachings and learn about upcoming events and Israel tours.

You can also find Rabbi Jason on Facebook:
https://www.facebook.com/rabbijasonsobel/

Rabbi Jason's Torah portions are available on Facebook:
https://www.facebook.com/groups/226402885216317/

For speaking engagements contact: info@fusionglobal.org

NOTES

NOTES

NOTES

NOTES

NOTES